SIERRA SMUCKER, TEAGUE RUDER,
STACEY YI, COREEN FARRIS

Veteran Single Parents

Surviving but Not Thriving

For more information on this publication, visit **www.rand.org/t/RRA1363-6**.

About RAND

The RAND Corporation is a research organization that develops solutions to public policy challenges to help make communities throughout the world safer and more secure, healthier and more prosperous. RAND is nonprofit, nonpartisan, and committed to the public interest. To learn more about RAND, visit www.rand.org.

Research Integrity

Our mission to help improve policy and decisionmaking through research and analysis is enabled through our core values of quality and objectivity and our unwavering commitment to the highest level of integrity and ethical behavior. To help ensure our research and analysis are rigorous, objective, and nonpartisan, we subject our research publications to a robust and exacting quality-assurance process; avoid both the appearance and reality of financial and other conflicts of interest through staff training, project screening, and a policy of mandatory disclosure; and pursue transparency in our research engagements through our commitment to the open publication of our research findings and recommendations, disclosure of the source of funding of published research, and policies to ensure intellectual independence. For more information, visit www.rand.org/about/research-integrity.

RAND's publications do not necessarily reflect the opinions of its research clients and sponsors.

Published by the RAND Corporation, Santa Monica, Calif.
© 2024 RAND Corporation
RAND® is a registered trademark.

Library of Congress Cataloging-in-Publication Data is available for this publication.
ISBN: 978-1-9774-1287-4

Cover: Kirsten Davis/peopleimages.com/Adobe Stock.

About This Report

The demographics of the veteran population are changing. Veterans who served after September 11, 2001 (post-9/11 veterans), are more likely to be female and identify as a person of color than their older counterparts. They are also more likely to be raising children, many of them without support from a partner. This report provides a comprehensive look at the financial, physical, and mental health of veteran single parents. We conclude by providing concrete recommendations on policies and programs that can better support veteran single parents and their children.

RAND Epstein Veterans Policy Research Institute

The RAND Epstein Family Veterans Policy Research Institute was established in 2021 with a generous gift from Daniel J. Epstein through the Epstein Family Foundation. The institute is dedicated to conducting innovative, evidence-based research and analysis to improve the lives of those who have served in the U.S. military. Building on decades of interdisciplinary expertise at the RAND Corporation, the institute prioritizes creative, equitable, and inclusive solutions and interventions that meet the needs of diverse veteran populations while engaging and empowering those who support them. For more information about the RAND Epstein Family Veterans Policy Research Institute, visit veterans.rand.org.

Funding

Funding for this publication was made possible by a generous gift from Daniel J. Epstein through the Epstein Family Foundation, which established the RAND Epstein Family Veterans Policy Research Institute in 2021.

Acknowledgments

We are incredibly grateful to the veterans who shared their stories with us for this report. Their honesty and willingness to spend time speaking with us was an enormous gift without which this report would not have been possible. We are also grateful to our excellent reviewers, Gary Bowen and Lynsay Ayer who provided us with constructive and supportive feedback to improve the report.

Summary

The changing demographics of the military demand that policymakers pay greater attention to veteran parents, particularly mothers. Women represent the fastest-growing population in the veteran community (Holder, 2010). Currently, women make up about 10 percent of the overall veteran population, and that percentage is expected to increase by 50 percent by 2035 (U.S. Department of Veterans Affairs [VA], 2017). Despite these statistics, few studies have focused on the impact of veteran status, gender, and parenthood on well-being outcomes and access to care (e.g., VA, 2017). This study expands our knowledge of the current experience of veteran single parents in the United States by answering the following research questions:

1. What are the demographic characteristics of veterans who served after September 11, 2001 (post-9/11 veteran) single parents, and how do they compare with veteran coupled parents and nonveteran single parents?
2. How do veteran single parents compare with nonveteran single parents and veteran coupled parents in terms of financial stability?
3. How do veteran single parents compare with nonveteran single parents and veteran parents in terms of mental and physical health and health care access?

Summary of Findings

Our analysis revealed that nearly 300,000 veteran parents identify as single. There were over 2.5 million veterans between the ages of 18 and 59 who identified as a parent of a child under 18 years of age between 2016 and 2020. Of those 2.5 million veterans, about 12 percent (294,677) identified as a single parent. For comparison, nearly 11 million nonveterans, or about 18 percent of nonveteran parents, identified as a single parent during the same span of time.

These veteran single parents are three times more likely than veteran coupled parents to identify as female and two times more likely than veteran coupled parents to identify as Black. Among veteran single parents, 42.8 percent identify as female, compared with only 13.9 percent of veteran coupled parents. Demographic data also show that 24.0 percent of veteran single parents identify as Black, compared with only 11.9 percent of veteran coupled parents.

Veteran single parents have a median personal income that is $18,000 less than that of veteran coupled parents. Median *personal* income of veteran single parents was $42,000, compared with that of veteran coupled parents ($60,000). In addition, median *household* income of veteran coupled parents was $102,000, which is significantly greater than that of veteran single parents ($58,580). Veteran single parents are also more likely than veteran coupled parents to experience food insecurity and less likely than veteran coupled parents to own a home.

Veteran single parents are more likely than veteran coupled parents to be enrolled in higher education. Just over 13 percent (13.1 percent) of veteran single parents reported being enrolled in higher education, compared with 10.7 percent of veteran coupled parents. In addition, veteran single parents were more likely than veteran coupled parents to be currently employed and enrolled in school (8.7 percent versus 7.9 percent, respectively).

Black female veteran single parents are more likely than veteran single parents of any other race and gender intersection to be enrolled in higher education. Female veteran single parents are more than twice as likely as their male counterparts to be enrolled in higher education (19.1 percent versus 8.6 percent, respectively). Analysis of race and gender intersections revealed that Black female veteran single parents are most likely to be enrolled in higher education (24.1 percent), followed by 20.1 percent of Hispanic female veteran single parents, 17.8 percent of Other Race female veteran single parents, and 15.2 percent of White female veteran single parents.

One example of a policy that should help close the gap between veteran coupled parents and veteran single parents, but does not always succeed, is the G.I. Bill. Veteran parents are using their G.I. Bill benefits. Indeed, a higher percentage of veteran single parents reported being enrolled in school than veteran coupled parents (13 percent versus 10 percent). Black and Hispanic veteran single mothers reported the highest rates of school enrollment (25 percent and 20 percent, respectively). Veteran single mothers are also more likely than veteran single fathers to be enrolled in school while simultaneously employed (13 percent versus 6 percent). However, qualitative interviews with veteran single parents pursuing higher education revealed significant barriers to using G.I. Bill benefits. Almost all interviewees discussed the difficulty of affording child care, working, and managing academic workload simultaneously. Specific aspects of the G.I. Bill were also burdensome for veteran single parents, particularly requirements to attend one class in-person to receive full housing benefits.

Recommendations

To reach parity with veteran coupled parents, veteran single parents need greater financial support when transitioning out of the military and into civilian jobs or education. Without support from another parent, veteran single parents likely have even greater demands on their time (full-time child-rearing) and resources (only one income) than veteran coupled parents. The fact that parents from ethnic and racial minority groups and woman veteran single parents face greater hardship than their White and male counterparts after leaving the military suggests that broader systemic inequalities in the United States also negatively affect veterans. Policies designed to support veteran single parents can improve equity in services, support, and outcomes for all veterans. Our recommendations are as follows:

- **Target transition services for veteran single parents as a unique group.** Veteran single parents might need additional guidance on career paths that allow them to balance family and career, affordable child care options, and information about how to apply for benefits, such as SNAP and other financial resources, as they transition out of the service. Although women are more likely to be single mothers than men are to be single fathers, half of all veteran single parents are men, so these efforts should be gender-inclusive and welcoming to single fathers. Research on nonveteran parents suggest that single fathers and fathers, more generally, feel alienated from professional services (e.g., education, health care) when seeking support for their children (Coles, 2015). Our veteran interviewees expressed similar barriers to support.

- **Provide federal financial support for child care for veterans.** Although there are many benefits offered to veterans who care for others (e.g., VA Dependent Parent Program) or family members of veterans (e.g., surviving spouse and child benefits), a limited number of programs and policies support veterans who are parents. Interestingly, there is a program that helps VA employees who are parents that earn below a certain income threshold for child care (VA Child Care Subsidy Program) but no similar program that specifically helps veterans with young children. Nongovernmental organizations like the Foundation for Women Warriors attempt to support woman veterans who need child care but are unable to extend these services to all veterans who need them. The demand for services from the Foundation for Women Warriors underlines the need for greater access to such services provided, ideally, by the VA and federal government.

- **Provide support for single parents in higher education.** We found that a relatively high percentage of the most financially insecure families headed by veteran singles were enrolled in higher education. These statistics suggest a commitment among veteran single parents to improve their future income levels and career trajectories to benefit themselves and their families. However, juggling school and being a full-time parent presents high barriers to completing education and fully using G.I. Bill benefits guaranteed to veterans. Key components of the G.I. Bill make completing a degree difficult for veteran single parents. By adjusting in-person requirements, waiving withdrawal penalties, and increasing the affordability of part-time degree participation, single parents could benefit from higher education as much as veteran coupled parents and veterans without children do (see Yi and Smucker [2024] for a deeper dive on this topic).

- **Provide mental health care for veteran single mothers.** Veteran single mothers reported higher rates of poor mental health than their male counterparts. Our analysis of survey data cannot tell us why this might be. However, given the higher rates of financial insecurity among women (especially women from minority ethnic and racial backgrounds) in our study, higher rates of financial insecurity might be related to poorer mental health outcomes for women. Other research also finds that woman veterans are more likely to have experienced military sexual trauma, depression, anxiety, and other common mental health disorders, which could contribute to this difference (Adams et al., 2021). Ensuring that single mothers have access to mental health support could help not only mothers but also their children.

- **Encourage single fathers to seek out primary care.** Veteran single fathers reported lower rates of health care seeking than did single mothers. These findings follow research that suggests single fathers are less likely to seek out health and behavioral health services for their children (Coles, 2015). Although our data cannot determine exactly why this is, it might be that fathers are less likely than mothers to engage in help seeking. Existing research finds that men are less likely to engage in help-seeking behaviors than women, especially for mental health concerns (Nam et al., 2010), and fathers also struggle to engage support resources (Ghaleiha et al., 2022). Ensuring that veteran single fathers are encouraged to access primary care could improve their long-term outcomes and ability to care for their children.

Future Research

This analysis raises many questions about the experience of veteran single parents. One central question is: What is driving differences in financial well-being and physical and mental health among veteran single parents, veteran coupled parents, and nonveteran parents? Although the present analysis provided some explanations based on existing research, our approach cannot determine whether such demographic characteristics as age and gender or military experience are driving differences among groups. Going forward, we hope to develop analyses that include the same or similar data but use more-advanced statistical analyses to isolate outcomes most associated with veteran and marital status.

Our intersectional analysis highlighted the importance of drilling down into subgroups to understand the unique issues facing veteran parents. We found significant reported food insecurity among mothers who identified as Other Race (Indian, Alaska Native, Asian, Native Hawaiian, Other Pacific Islander, or two or more races); over one-third reported that their children received free or reduced-price lunches in the past 30 days. We also found that Hispanic single mothers were struggling with mental health more than other groups and that Black single fathers were more likely to report issues accessing health care than other groups. Future research could continue to focus on these groups to identify their unique experiences and policies that would better meet their needs.

Finally, future research should unpack how different child custody or child support arrangements affect veteran single parents. It seems likely that certain custody arrangements and child support levels could influence the financial pressure faced by veteran single parents. Moreover, veterans might have unique child custody arrangements if they were single parents prior to or during their military career. Because about 5 percent of active-duty service members identify as a single parent, the experience of single parenthood in the military and as a veteran could involve compounding issues, especially if children were sent to live with another relative while the parent deployed (Military OneSource, undated). Future survey or qualitative work could better capture how child care arrangements mediate the outcomes documented in this report.

Limitations

Our analysis is limited in several ways. First, we did not adjust for demographic characteristics in our analysis. This means that the differences we saw between parents and veterans could be highly correlated with other factors that we did not account for. As we mentioned previously, we viewed this analysis as a first step toward understanding the unique circumstances that drive veteran single parents' experiences and account for differences between their well-being and those of veteran coupled parents and nonveteran single parents.

Another limitation is our sample. Although the ACS and BRFSS provide one of the most representative samples of veterans, our analysis focused on averages from a broad period (2016–2021), which could mask more-subtle variation in results in specific years. For example, shutdowns related to the coronavirus disease 2019 pandemic likely excaerbated child care challenges during the study period. We were also limited by information collected by the ACS and BRFSS. We did not know, for example, whether individuals receive or pay child support while raising children on their own. We also did not know whether children were born before the person became a veteran or after. Having children while in the military or before military service has unique impacts on children, especially children with single parents (e.g., when a parent deploys). Qualitative data could get closer to unpacking these relationships. We also did not compare how the age of the child mediated parent outcomes, which limited our ability to understand differences in outcomes across newer and more-established parents.

Finally, we captured only qualitative data from a narrow group of veterans: veteran single parents who are or were previously enrolled in higher education. As a result, the qualitative component has limited validity outside that narrow group. However, understanding barriers veteran single parents face when trying to use benefits associated with military service sheds light on reasons why veteran single parents do not use their higher education benefits. As many of our interviewees attested, they often relied on outside help from family or charity to get through their education while raising children on their own. We can infer that there are many veteran single parents who do not have access to such resources and, consequently, never enroll in school. Future research should engage in more qualitative data collection across a broader range of veteran single parents.

Contents

Tables

CHAPTER 1

Introduction

The changing demographics of the military demand that policymakers pay greater attention to veteran parents, particularly mothers. Women represent the fastest-growing population in the veteran community (Holder, 2010). Currently, women make up about 10 percent of the overall veteran population, and that percentage is expected to increase by 50 percent by 2035 (U.S. Department of Veterans Affairs [VA], 2017). Despite these statistics, few studies have focused on the impact of veteran status, gender, and parenthood on well-being outcomes and access to care (e.g., VA, 2017).

The limited studies on veteran parents suggest that woman veterans are more likely to be single mothers than male veterans are to be single fathers (Hanson and Woods, 2016; Wounded Warrior Project [WWP], 2021; Holder, 2010). The most recent representative study used American Community Survey (ACS) data from 2013 to 2014 and found that 11 percent of veteran families were single-parent households, and 57 percent of that 11 percent were headed by women (Hanson and Woods, 2016). A more recent investigation from 2020 surveyed a subset of wounded, ill, and injured women veterans registered with WWP who served after September 11, 2001 (post-9/11), and found that, among women veterans with children, 49 percent were single mothers (WWP, 2021).

These investigations found that parents, particularly single parents, face significant obstacles to mental and physical well-being, as well as financial security. Hanson and Woods (2016) found that single parents differed from households with two parents (married or unmarried) in terms of education (single parents had less education), employment (single parents had higher rates of unemployment), and income (single parents had higher rates of poverty). Hanson and Woods concluded that, "Although only 11 percent of [veteran] families are single parents, these more than 100,000 families appear to be the most vulnerable" (2016, p. 25). The survey of women registered with WWP had similar findings and stressed that women veterans faced significant financial stress and that access to care was limited by their child care, work, and family responsibilities (WWP, 2021). These initial investigations suggest that single-parent households might need greater and different support than dual-parent households. Moreover, woman veterans might be disproportionately affected by the barriers to care that affect single-parent households.

This study builds on existing literature and expands our knowledge of the current experience of veteran single parents in the United States by answering the following research questions:

- What are the demographic characteristics of post-9/11 veteran single parents and how do they compare with veteran coupled parents and nonveteran single parents?
- How do veteran single parents compare with nonveteran single parents and veteran coupled parents in terms of financial stability?
- How do veteran single parents compare with nonveteran single parents and veteran coupled parents in terms of mental and physical health and health care access?

We also explore the differences across these factors by race, ethnicity, and gender.

Brief Review of the Literature

Single parents face significant difficulties across a variety of well-being indicators. Because women are more likely to be single parents than men, most studies of single parents focus on women. Single mothers report greater financial difficulties, social isolation, and child care responsibilities compared with their married counterparts (Craig, 2006; Pearlin and Johnson, 1977). Married mothers often report better mental health when compared with single mothers because of greater access to support from their partner financially and for child care (Cairney et al., 1999; Cairney et al., 2003; Davies, Avison, and McApline, 1997; Wang, 2004). Furthermore, mothers in two-parent households report more-stable, better-paid employment than single mothers (Mattingly, Smith, and Bean, 2011; Wu and Eamon, 2011). When parents have irregular work patterns and employment instability, children can experience negative impacts on development and well-being (Hepburn, 2018; Kalil and Ziol-Guest, 2005; Lleras, 2008). These findings likely characterize differences between veteran single parents and veteran coupled parents: Veteran single parents likely have less regular support for child care and rearing than veteran coupled parents.

However, there are reasons veteran single parents might have better mental, physical, and financial outcomes than nonveteran single parents. First, accession requirements to join the military create a selection bias where veterans are more likely to have high school diplomas; not have a criminal record; and be, generally, physically healthy, which could lead to better outcomes than for the general nonveteran population (McLaughlin, Nielsen, and Waller, 2008). Additionally, veterans are older than nonveteran single parents, on average (see Table 2.1 of this report), which typically comes with greater financial resources from savings and work experience. Moreover, veterans benefit from several policies that provide education benefits, pensions, and disability benefits, likely improving their financial security compared with nonveteran single parents (Bowen, Orthner, and Zimmerman, 1993; Angrist, 1993).

On the other hand, veterans face unique circumstances related to physical and mental health that most nonveteran single parents are likely not exposed to. Veterans who served in Operation Enduring Freedom and Operation Iraqi Freedom have elevated rates of the invisible wounds of war, such as posttraumatic stress disorder and traumatic brain injury (Tanielian et al., 2008). Improved weapons and armor mean that service members are more likely to survive serious injuries than in the past, but this reduction in deaths is linked to a rise in the number of amputations and serious physical injuries that require lifelong care (Tanielian et al., 2008). Long-term caretaking often falls to the spouses, parents, and, later, adult children of the veteran, who often face multiple sources of emotional, financial, and family stress (Ramchand et al., 2014). Moreover, children whose parents are in the military, especially those who deploy, could experience trauma that could lead to greater challenges for children and parents later in life (Sheppard, Malatras, and Israel, 2010; Trautmann, Alhusen, and Gross, 2015).

Because veterans face similar obstacles to those of single civilian parents but have access to benefits similar to and share experiences with veteran coupled parents, we compared veteran single parents with both groups to understand how veteran single parents differ from their coupled and nonveteran counterparts. Based on existing research, our central hypothesis is that veteran single parents will report lower financial, physical, and mental well-being than veteran coupled parents. This is because coupled parents, in general, can share financial and child care responsibilities or pay for outside child care, giving both more time to also take care of their own physical and mental health than veteran single parents.

However, we also hypothesize that veteran single parents will report greater financial well-being than nonveteran single parents. We suspect that veteran single parents will have greater access to financial support (through military pensions and disability benefits) than nonveteran single parents. It could be that veteran single parents have worse physical and mental health than nonveteran single parents because of their service in the military and any physical and mental wounds they sustained during that time. However, veteran single parents' greater access to health care through their military benefits could ameliorate some of these differences if they exist.

This report builds on the existing research on veteran single parents by leveraging a larger and more representative dataset and delving into a more comprehensive list of outcomes than previous studies. We also break down the results by gender and race. With the increasing diversity of the veteran population, it is important to understand whether outcomes are similar or distinct across subgroups, particularly those who have been found to face barriers to success in and after military service (e.g., women [Robinson and O'Hanlon, 2020] and minority groups [Carlson et al., 2018]). We highlight key differences across these subgroups and their intersections (e.g., Black veteran single mothers, Hispanic veteran single fathers) and provide the detailed data for all these interactions in the appendix. By considering the unique experiences of veteran single parents by gender and racial identity (and the intersection of both), we provide a nuanced account of the well-being of veteran single parents.

Results

In general, we found evidence for our original hypotheses: Veteran single parents were less well off financially, mentally, and physically than veteran coupled parents but were better off than nonveteran single parents. However, some interesting deviations from that pattern emerged. We found variation in these patterns when we looked at subgroups of veteran single parents across race, ethnicity, and gender. Our qualitative work also revealed that policy support for veterans—specifically educational support from the G.I. Bill—lacked consideration for the unique experience of single parents. This lack of consideration created gaps in support that could limit the positive impact of such policies on the well-being of veteran single parents.

It is important to note that these differences are likely due, in part, to compositional differences across groups like age and education. However, it is not the goal of this report to link outcomes to individual characteristics but rather describe the population as a whole and highlight some factors that could drive differences. Therefore, we focused on descriptive statistics and did not use regression analysis. Future studies could investigate causal relationships between demographic factors and outcomes for veteran parents.

Organization of This Report

We summarize the results of our investigation by outcome. In Chapter 2, we begin by outlining our methodology and the demographic characteristics of veteran and nonveteran single parents. In Chapter 3, we discuss the financial health and stability across veteran parents and nonveteran single parents and consider the differences in these outcomes by race and gender. In Chapter 4, we turn to mental and physical health outcomes, as well as access to health care across parent and veteran status, again considering the differences in these outcomes by race and gender. In Chapter 5, we discuss the emerging theme of access to and use of educational benefits, such as the G.I. Bill. In Chapter 6, we offer concluding remarks and recommendations for policymakers, advocates, and military leadership interested in improving the lives of veteran single parents. Finally, in the appendix, we provide a comprehensive set of tables that describe the differences in these outcomes across race, ethnicity, gender, and the intersection of these identities.

CHAPTER 2

Methodology and Demographic Overview

We answered our three core research questions using 2016–2020 data from the ACS, Current Population Survey (CPS) Food Security Supplement (FSS), and Behavioral Risk Factor Surveillance System (BRFSS) (U.S. Census Bureau, 2016–2020; U.S. Census Bureau and U.S. Bureau of Labor Statistics, 2016–2020; Centers for Disease Control and Prevention [CDC], 2016–2020). We also incorporated qualitative interviews with a targeted group of veteran single parents in higher education.

The ACS is an ongoing survey of the Census Bureau that collects a rich set of information on the U.S. population. The Census releases two public-use versions of the ACS: the Summary Files (ACS-SF) and the Public Use Microdata Sample (ACS-PUMS). The ACS-SF is a limited set of tables that represents the full population. We used these data to answer general questions, but most analyses stratifying by veteran status required use of the individual-level data in the ACS-PUMS. To increase the sample size, particularly of the veteran population, we used the five-year ACS-PUMS covering 2016–2020.

The CPS is a joint effort by the U.S. Census Bureau and U.S. Bureau of Labor Statistics used to create labor force statistics. The base survey is fielded monthly, and different supplemental surveys are posed to subpopulations each month. In December, the FSS generates scores of household-level food insecurity. For consistency with the ACS, we pooled five years of CPS-FSS data from 2016–2020.

The BRFSS is a large survey collected by the CDC that measures health-related risk behaviors, chronic health conditions, use of preventive services, and access to health care. In addition to including a core group of questions, it contains several optional modules that are fielded in a subset of years and states. For consistency, we pooled five years of BRFSS data from 2016–2020.

We limited the sample to parents aged 18 to 59 who had children under the age of 17 living with them full time. Both the CPS and BRFSS are limited to the civilian noninstitutional population. For consistency, we removed active-duty service members from the ACS populations, which affects only the composition of the nonveteran population.

We also conducted 11 semistructured interviews with student veteran single parents. We recruited this group through a partnership with the Student Veterans of America organization, which sent an email to its members describing the study and asking for interested participants. We then contacted the individuals who indicated they were willing to participate. Each participant was offered $50 for their time. The interview questions were designed to elicit descriptions of interviewees' experiences with an eye toward identifying barriers experienced when they pursued their degrees. The interviews were approved by RAND's Human Subjects Protection Committee.

The interview sample consisted of five men and six women who were raising between one and five children and were currently attending or had attended college in the past five years. Those interviewed typically started pursuing higher education a few years after leaving the military, and one of the interviewees was a nonveteran school administrator whose job is to support student veterans. The children ranged in age from infants to teenagers during the time the veteran was enrolled.[1] Although the sample was relatively small, we reached saturation with our qualitative data quickly; veterans highlighted the same core factors that facilitated or impeded their pursuit of higher education within the first six interviews.

All interviews were transcribed and uploaded to Dedoose qualitative analysis software for coding. One researcher coded the interviews for emergent themes, including policy considerations and barriers and facilitators to success. A second researcher then double-checked each interview for missing or incorrect codes. All disagreements in coding were discussed between the two researchers until consensus was established.

With these mixed-methods data, we answered key questions about the financial and health needs of veteran parents, particularly veteran single parents. Our findings and recommendations will help to better inform policymakers' decisions on how to allocate resources offered to veterans in accordance with their contemporary needs.

Definitions

We used the following definitions in our analysis.

Single parent. We defined single parent in our ACS data as (1) a person aged 18 years or older with a child under 18 years and no spouse or partner present or (2) a parent in a parent-child subfamily (living in another adult's home). In the CPS, we defined a single parent as an individual aged 18 years or older living with their own child under 18 years of age with any of the following marital statuses: absent, widowed, divorced, separated, or never married. In BRFSS, a single parent is defined as an individual age 18 or older living in a household with at least one child under 18 years of age with any of the following marital statuses: divorced, widowed, separated, or never married.[2]

Veteran. In the ACS and CPS, a veteran is an individual who served on active duty in the U.S. military in the past but is not serving now. In BRFSS, a veteran is any individual who has ever served on active duty. BRFSS is limited to a civilian, noninstitutional population, so it will not include individuals currently serving on active duty.

---

[1] We did not ask detailed information about children in the interviews to preserve their privacy.

[2] It is possible that these parents have some kind of co-parenting relationship with the other parent, but it is not possible to differentiate between custody arrangements in these data.

Measures

Financial Measures

Income and employment. We used two measures to assess income in the ACS. First, we looked at a self-reported measure of income, both individual and total household. Note that these payments might include child support payments to single parents. We also used a self-reported measure for employment in which respondents can state that they are working full time, working part time, or not in the labor force. These measures provide a foundational picture of the access to resources and financial stability of each set of parents.

Financial public assistance. Use of state-funded aid programs can also tell us about the financial well-being of parents. Families that qualify for state-based assistance meet certain thresholds deemed by policymakers to indicate financial need. To measure support from state-based programs, we included a few indicators provided by the ACS. Social Security Income (SSI) is a federal program that provides monthly payments to the elderly and children with a disability and individuals with limited incomes. Public assistance includes all income received from state or local welfare programs, such as Temporary Assistance for Needy Families, General Assistance, and Emergency Assistance. It does not include assistance received from private charities for food, rent, education, child care, transportation, or energy costs.

Food insecurity. Food security is also a critical component of financial well-being. A family might have an income above certain thresholds for poverty, but other factors could undermine their ability to access food for themselves and their children. A lack of access to food puts families at risk for a host of negative outcomes (Johnson and Markowitz, 2018). We used two measures to assess food insecurity. First, we calculated the percentage of each group that reported receiving Supplemental Nutrition Assistance Program (SNAP) benefits. SNAP is the largest federal nutrition assistance program and provides benefits to eligible low-income individuals and families. Eligibility requirements vary by state but generally relate to bank balance amounts. Thus, a high rate of SNAP receipt suggests that a high proportion of the group has a low bank balance and a need for food assistance, but a low rate of SNAP receipt does not necessarily suggest no need for food assistance. For example, a low rate of SNAP receipt in a population with low incomes could suggest that members of the group do not know how to access this resource or believe they do not qualify. It is possible that veterans might not believe they qualify for this program because they might have some supplemental income. To help clarify between these two possibilities, we included the food insecurity measure from the BRFSS, which indicates whether a household was uncertain of having or unable to acquire enough food to meet the needs of all their members because they had insufficient money or other resources for food. Together, these measures present a picture of the experience of food insecurity across these groups.

Housing. We interpreted homeownership as a sign of financial stability and long-term security. Owning a stable asset like a house can not only provide long-term housing at lower rates than renting but can also fund future retirement plans if the asset is sold or rented out. We also include a measure of *living with parents*. This measure captured whether the veteran or nonveteran parent reported living in their parents' home or whether their parent included the veteran and their children as members of their household.[3] Additionally, we looked at the percentage of income spent on housing (whether mortgage or renting costs) across veterans and nonveterans with children. Individuals who spend over 30 percent on housing are considered *house burdened* according to the U.S. Department of Housing and Urban Development (Kimberlin, 2019). We used this cutoff to assess the housing security across veteran parents and nonveteran single parents.

Mental and Physical Health Measures

Mental and physical health. We used self-reported measures from the BRFSS to examine the differences in mental and physical health across parents. Specifically, we used measures that ask participants, "How many days last month was your [mental health/physical health] not good?" and "How many days last month did you have poor physical or mental health?" We also used a measure of general health through which participants could report "excellent" to "poor" general health.

    Health care use. We also included measures of health care access and use. The first measure was a self-reported indicator of health insurance from BRFSS. We also included respondents' reporting of access to a personal doctor and whether they attended a routine checkup in the past year. The final measure asked whether the participant could not see a doctor in the past year because of cost.

Demographic Characteristics of Veteran Parents and Nonveterans

Between 2016 and 2020, there were over 2.5 million veterans between 18 and 59 who identified as a parent of a child under 18 years of age. Of those 2.5 million, about 12 percent (294,677) identified as single parents. Conversely, nearly 11 million nonveterans identified as a single parent during this time out of a population of about 59 million parents between the ages of 18 and 59 (or 18 percent). Table 2.1 outlines the demographic differences between these populations.

    Veteran parents, whether single or in a couple, were more like each other than they were like nonveteran single parents, demographically. To start, veteran parents were older than nonveteran single parents: Most veteran parents reported ages between 30 and 49 years old

---

[3] Our interpretation of this measure was that a person who is living in their parents' home likely does not have the resources or financial capacity to purchase their own home and build equity, which could benefit them long term. Although it is also possible that some percentage of these individuals chose to live in their parents' home despite financial stability, looking at this measure along with others helped us triangulate data points and develop a deeper picture of veterans' experience.

while nonveteran single parents were more likely to be between 18 and 29 years old; the majority were under the age of 39.

Across race and ethnicity, however, veteran single parents were more likely to identify as Black, non-Hispanic than veteran coupled parents (24.0 percent versus 11.9 percent). Nearly 70 percent of veteran coupled parents identified as White, non-Hispanic compared with only 56.2 percent of veteran single parents. About one-quarter of nonveteran single parents identified as Black (26.0 percent) while 42.1 percent identified as White, non-Hispanic. About 13 percent of all veteran parents (both single and in a couple) identified as Hispanic compared with 24.8 percent of nonveteran single parents.

Very few parents in our sample identified as a race or ethnicity outside White, Black, and Hispanic. The next most common was Asian, non-Hispanic, which included 2.8 percent of nonveteran single parents, 1.5 percent of veteran single parents, and 2.3 percent of veteran coupled parents. Less than 1 percent of parents in our sample identified as Native Hawaiian or Pacific Islander, non-Hispanic (0.2 percent of nonveteran single parents, 0.3 percent of veteran single parents, and 0.3 percent of veteran coupled parents); about 1 percent identified as American Indian or Alaskan Native, non-Hispanic (1.1 percent of nonveteran single parents, 1.1 percent of veteran single parents, and 0.7 percent of veteran coupled parents); and between 2 and 4 percent identified as two or more races (2.8 percent of nonveteran single parents, 3.8 percent of veteran single parents, and 3.1 percent of veteran coupled parents). Under 0.5 percent of parents selected "Other" for race (0.3 percent of nonveteran single parents, 0.3 percent of veteran single parents, and 0.2 percent of veteran coupled parents).

One key demographic difference across the groups was self-identified gender of the parent. In keeping with the literature on single parenthood, most nonveteran single parents identified as women (81.5 percent). However, among veteran single parents, just over 40 percent identified as women (42.8 percent), which means over half of veteran single parents identified as male. This difference is likely explained by the high proportion of men who enter the military in the first place, leading to a higher rate of single fathers in this population. Thus, although women make up less than half of veteran single parents, this equates to a higher proportion of women veteran single parents compared with their male counterparts: 26 percent of veteran mothers are single parents compared with 11 percent of veteran fathers. Conversely, among veteran coupled parents, only 13 percent identify as women.

There are also differences in education attainment across parent groups. Veteran single parents reported completing more education than nonveteran single parents. Veteran single parents were less likely to report having less than a high school degree compared with nonveteran single parents (13.9 percent versus 2.7 percent) and less likely to report having only a high school level education compared with nonveteran single parents (29.7 percent versus 19.6 percent). Moreover, almost half of veteran single parents reported attending some college (48.2 percent) compared with only about one-third of nonveteran single parents (36.3 percent). Almost one-third of veteran single parents have a college degree (29.5 percent) compared with one-fifth of nonveteran single parents (20.2 percent).

TABLE 2.1

Demographic Characteristics of Parents Across Veteran and Marital Status

| | Nonveteran Single Parent (n = 10,808,338) | Veteran | |
Demographic Characteristic		Single Parent (n = 294,677)	Coupled Parent (n = 2,228,831)
Age (%)[a, b]			
18 to 29 years	24.3	10.3	8.0
30 to 39 years	37.0	35.6	33.4
40 to 49 years	29.1	36.6	39.0
50 to 59 years	9.7	17.5	19.5
Race and ethnicity (%)[a, b]			
Black, non-Hispanic	26.0	24.0	11.9
White, non-Hispanic	42.1	56.2	69.1
Asian, non-Hispanic	2.8	1.5	2.3
Native Hawaiian or Pacific Islander, non-Hispanic	0.2	0.3	0.3
American Indian or Alaskan Native, non-Hispanic	1.1	1.1	0.7
Two or more races, non-Hispanic	2.8	3.8	3.1
Other, non-Hispanic	0.3	0.3	0.2
Hispanic	24.8	12.9	12.4
Gender (%)[a, b]			
Woman	81.5	42.8	13.9
Man	18.5	57.2	86.1
Educational attainment (%)[a, b]			
Less than high school degree	13.9	2.7	1.6
High school graduate or GED	29.7	19.6	18.6
Some college with no degree	36.3	48.2	43.5
Bachelor's degree or higher	20.1	29.5	36.3
Enrolled in higher education[a, b]	8.9	13.1	10.7
Average number of children[a, b]	1.7	1.6	1.9

SOURCE: ACS-PUMS five-year data from 2016–2020.

NOTE: GED = General Education Development.

[a] Denotes significant difference between veteran and nonveteran single parents at the < 0.01 level.

[b] Denotes significant difference between veteran single parents and veteran coupled parents at the < 0.01 level.

Veteran coupled parents reported attaining higher levels of education than both groups of single parents, although the greatest difference was seen in the attainment of a college degree: 36.3 percent of veteran coupled parents reported having a bachelor's degree or higher compared with only 29.5 percent of veteran single parents. However, veteran single parents reported higher rates of current school enrollment than both groups (13.1 percent of veteran single parents compared with 8.9 percent of nonveteran single parents and 10.7 percent of veteran coupled parents), meaning, over time, the ratios of educational attainment between these populations could change. All groups reported similar numbers of children, on average (between 1.6 and 1.9).

In sum, veteran single parents are more like their nonveteran counterparts across racial and ethnic lines but look more like other veteran parents in terms of age and educational attainment. Veteran single parents differ greatly from nonveteran single parents and other veteran parents in their gender identity: Just under half of veteran single parents identify as women, and the remaining half identify as men.

CHAPTER 3

Financial Well-Being of Veteran Single Parents

Although limited in number, the existing surveys that examine veteran financial well-being suggest that veterans might have higher levels of financial well-being than the average U.S. adult (Consumer Financial Protection Bureau Office of Servicemember Affairs, 2019). These findings could be explained by the benefits, including health care, educational benefits, subsidized child care, and pensions, that military service confers to service members and veterans that improve their financial situations. Moreover, as previously mentioned, accession requirements to join the military create a selection bias where veterans are more likely to have high school diplomas and not have a criminal record, which could lead to better outcomes than the general nonveteran population. However, there are some ways in which elements of military service could put veterans at a disadvantage to their nonveteran peers, including frequent relocation while in the service, leading to limited spouse employment opportunities and a lack of community support; war-related trauma; and potentially difficult transitions into nonveteran life.

Table 3.1 provides an overview of our measures of financial security across parents by veteran and marital status. The result of this analysis supports our original hypothesis that veteran single parents will face greater financial pressure than veteran coupled parents but less pressure than nonveteran single parents. It is important to note that these results (and those that follow) do not control for demographic differences between groups that could be correlated with different levels of financial well-being. For example, on average, men are paid higher rates than women for similar work (Bishu and Alkadry, 2017). This could be driving differences in income between veteran parents and nonveteran single parents because veterans are far more likely to be male than nonveteran single parents. Age could also play a role. Older people typically make more money than younger people because they have been in the labor force longer and could have accumulated assets (Ozhamaratli, Kitov, and Barucca, 2022). Veteran single parents are older, on average, than nonveteran single parents, which could explain some of the difference in income between the two groups. The same is true for other measures of financial welfare.

To address this possibility, we conducted additional analyses adjusting for age, gender, race, and educational attainment in our primary analyses (across veteran, nonveteran, and

TABLE 3.1

Financial Security Across Veteran and Nonveteran Parents

Demographic Characteristic	Nonveteran Single Parent	Veteran	
		Single Parent	Coupled Parent
Median personal income[a, b]	$24,000	$42,000	$60,000
Median household income[a, b]	$42,500	$58,580	$102,000
Percentage receiving the following forms of assistance			
Self-employment income[a, b]	5.6	4.8	5.9
SSI[a, b]	3.8	2.4	0.9
Public assistance income[a, b]	6.1	2.9	0.6
Retirement income[a, c]	2.3	13.0	12.3
SNAP benefits in past year[a, b]	37.1	18.4	7.6
No health insurance[a, b]	15.6	5.7	3.3
Food security (%)			
Living in a low food security household[b]	22.2	17.3	4.4
Living in a very low food security household[b]	5.5	5.4	1.1
Receipt of free or reduced-price lunch in past 30 days[a, b, d]	32.0	20.1	8.7
Use of food pantry in past 30 days[b]	11.7	8.5	2.4

SOURCE: ACS-PUMS five-year file, 2016–2020; CPS-FSS, 2016–2020.

[a] Denotes significant difference between veteran and nonveteran single parents at the < 0.01 level.

[b] Denotes significant difference between veteran single parents and veteran coupled parents at the < 0.01 level.

[c] In adjusted tables, the difference between veteran single parents and veteran coupled parents became significant at the < 0.01 level.

[d] After adjusting for age, race, gender, and educational attainment, the difference between veteran and nonveteran single parents became insignificant.

coupled status) and found that, in most cases, results held.[1] We highlight results that did change when adjusted in the tables below. We also discuss the interactions between race and gender and these measures later in the report to understand whether demographic factors are associated with different outcomes.

---

[1] We used the unadjusted rates in this report to focus on the experience of veteran single parents without trying to disentangle whether these experiences were because of their veteran status or their coupled status. Policy solutions to problems of veteran single parents should not solely focus on issues that stem specifically from their military experience but the totality of their lives. We note results that were statistically different after adjusting for the above characteristics in each of the following tables.

First, we examined the personal and family incomes reported by parents. These two indicators give us a sense of the annual funds on which parents can rely to cover living expenses. Looking first at median personal income, 50 percent of veteran single parents make less than $42,000. This number is $18,000 less for nonveteran single parents and $18,000 more for veteran coupled parents. Moving to total household income, veteran coupled parents report a median household income of $102,000, which is almost double that of veteran single parents. Veteran single parents have a median household income closer to that of nonveteran single parents: $58,580 for veteran single parents compared with $42,500 for nonveteran single parents.

Differences in total household income likely reflect the number of people working in the home (single parents will likely have one person working), but it does not explain the difference entirely. Many veteran coupled parents have only one person in the household working while the other provides child care. Moreover, personal income differences suggest that, regardless of dual income, veteran coupled parents make more money per year individually than veteran single parents.

Additionally, differences in reported income could stem from such demographic differences as gender and race. Nonveteran single parents are more likely to be women than veteran parents (40 percent more likely), and veteran single parents are more likely to be women than veteran coupled parents (30 percent more likely). These differences could explain some of the income differences across parent groups. Indeed, later in the analysis, we compare male and woman veteran single parents and find that the median income for veteran single mothers is $10,000 less than veteran single fathers (Table A.8 in the appendix). Race could also play a role: White parents, on average, have higher incomes than parents from racial and ethnic minority backgrounds. However, the racial and ethnic differences across these groups of parents is less striking than the gender differences. Veteran single parents are only slightly more likely to be White than nonveteran single parents and less likely to identify as Hispanic as nonveteran single parents. Compared with veteran coupled parents, veteran single parents are about 10 percent less likely to be White and 10 percent more likely to identify as Black (compared with 30 percent more likely to be female).

Next, we examined SSI and public assistance income, using it as another measure of the financial well-being of the family. Veteran single parents are more likely than veteran coupled parents to receive SSI (2.4 percent versus 0.9 percent) but less likely than nonveteran single parents to receive SSI (2.4 percent versus 3.8 percent). Similarly, veteran single parents are more likely than veteran coupled parents to receive public assistance income (2.9 percent versus 0.6 percent) but less likely than nonveteran single parents to receive it (2.9 percent versus 6.1 percent). All veteran parents receive retirement income at similar rates: 13.0 percent of veteran single parents and 12.3 percent of veteran coupled parents collect retirement income. However, only 2.3 percent of nonveteran single parents collect retirement income. This difference is likely because service members can draw on their pension funds earlier in their career than the typical nonveteran can. This could be another explanation for why veteran single parents are better off financially than nonveteran single parents: Support earned through their military service provides a buffer against financial strain typical among single parents in the general population. However, these supports do not close the financial gap between coupled and veteran single parents.

Next, we turned to food insecurity across parents. Nonveteran and veteran single parents are in a more precarious situation than veteran coupled parents. Nonveteran and veteran single parents are more likely to report living in a low food security household (22.2 percent and 17.3 percent, respectively) while only 4.4 percent of veteran coupled parents report it.[2] In total, 5.5 percent of nonveteran single parents and 5.4 percent of veteran single parents report living in a "very low" food security household compared with only 1.1 percent of veteran coupled parents. Children of nonveteran single parents and veteran single parents are more likely (32.0 percent and 20.1 percent, respectively) than children of veteran coupled parents (8.7 percent) to have qualified for free or reduced-priced lunch in the past 30 days. Looking at SNAP receipt, we found that nonveteran single parents were far more likely than veteran parents to receive SNAP. Over one-third (37.1 percent) of nonveteran single parents reported receiving SNAP benefits compared with only 18.4 percent of veteran single parents and only 7.6 percent of veteran coupled parents. Together, these results suggest that veteran and nonveteran single parents both face food insecurity, but nonveteran parents' SNAP uptake is far greater than that of veterans (nearly double the percentage of veteran single parents).

Next, we looked at housing. We interpreted homeownership as a sign of financial stability and long-term security because owning a stable asset like a house can not only provide long-term housing at lower rates than renting but can also fund future retirement plans if the asset is sold or rented out. We also included a measure of *living with parents*. This measure captured whether the veteran or nonveteran parent reported living in their parents' home or whether their parent included the veteran and their children as members of their household. Additionally, we looked at the percentage of income spent on housing (whether mortgage or renting costs) across veterans and nonveterans with children. Individuals who spend over 30 percent on housing are considered *house burdened* according to the U.S. Department of Housing and Urban Development (Kimberlin, 2019). We used this cutoff to assess the housing security across veteran parents and nonveteran single parents.

Following our hypothesis, data from the ACS (Table 3.2) suggest that veteran single parents are more likely than their nonveteran counterparts to own a home with a mortgage (43.3 percent versus 31.6 percent) but less likely than veteran coupled parents (65.5 percent) to do so. It follows that both groups of single parents are more likely to report renting a home than veteran coupled parents. Veteran single parents are much more likely to live in their parents' home than veteran coupled parents (16.6 percent versus 1.8 percent) but are less likely than nonveteran single parents (24.9 percent) to do so. Some veteran single parents might report living in a home with a mortgage or report being mortgage free when they are living in their parents' home. Living with parents could confer the dual benefit of free child care

---

[2] *Food insecurity* is defined as "the limited or uncertain availability of nutritionally adequate and safe foods, or limited or uncertain ability to acquire acceptable foods in socially acceptable ways" (Andersen, 1990).

TABLE 3.2

Housing Across Veteran and Nonveteran Parents

| | | Veterans | |
Characteristic	Nonveteran Single Parent	Single Parent	Coupled Parent
Homeownership (%)[a, b, c]			
Home owned with mortgage	31.6	43.3	65.5
Home owned free and clear	12.5	12.7	9.5
Home rented	55.9	44.0	25.0
Subfamily household (%)[a, b]			
Primary household	69.7	80.5	98.0
Living in parent household	24.9	16.6	1.8
Living in another household	5.4	2.8	0.2
Percentage of income spent on housing costs[a, b]			
< 10%	8.8	10.4	13.3
10–19.9%	20.1	26.4	41.7
20–29.9%	20.2	23.7	25.3
30–39.9%	14.1	13.8	9.2
40–49.9%	8.7	7.3	3.9
> 50%	23.8	15.5	5.5

SOURCE: ACS-PUMS five-year file, 2016–2020.

[a] Denotes significant difference between veteran and nonveteran single parents at the < 0.01 level.

[b] Denotes significant difference between veteran single parents and veteran coupled parents at the < 0.01 level.

[c] After adjusting for age, race, gender, and educational attainment, the difference between veteran and nonveteran single parents became insignificant.

and lower housing costs, making it an attractive option (if available) for single parents in general, including veteran single parents. These veterans may or may not pay rent to their family members. This possibility makes this measure of housing security difficult to interpret without qualitative data.

However, other measures of housing costs suggest that, despite higher rates of living with parents, veteran single parents spend a significant amount of their income on housing. Veteran single parents are more likely to spend over 30 percent of their income on housing than their coupled peers; 15.5 percent of veteran single parents spend over 50 percent of their income on housing. Comparatively, most veteran coupled parents spend less than 20 percent on housing, and only 5.5 percent of veteran coupled parents spend over 50 percent of their income on housing. Nonveteran single parents face higher costs than both, however; 23.8 percent of them spend more than 50 percent of their income on housing. These data, once again, support our hypothesis that veteran single parents face greater financial struggles than veteran coupled parents but are more secure than nonveteran single parents.

Employment rates across the groups were relatively similar. Outlined in Table 3.3, 77.0 percent of veteran single parents reported being currently employed compared with 75.2 percent of nonveteran single parents and 85.5 percent of veteran coupled parents. However, 18.3 percent of nonveteran single parents and 18.1 percent of veteran single parents reported not participating in the labor force and, consequently, not bringing in income; only 12.0 percent of veteran coupled parents reported not participating in the labor force. These results might explain why median incomes for veteran single parents are lower than veteran coupled parent median incomes and why veteran single parents might exit the labor market to provide child care. This result could also be linked to the fact that 13.1 percent of veteran single parents report higher education enrollment. However, veteran single parents were the most likely to be in school and working (8.7 percent), although they were only slightly more likely to do so than veteran coupled parents (7.9 percent) and nonveteran single parents (6.4 percent).

Considering Gender, Race, and Ethnicity in Financial Well-Being Indicators

We also analyzed these data across subgroups—including gender, race, and ethnic identity—with a focus on veteran single parents. The full tables can be found in the appendix. Here, we outline the notable differences that emerge when looking at the data with an intersectional lens.

TABLE 3.3

Employment Across Veteran and Nonveteran Parents

Characteristic	Nonveteran Single Parent	Veterans	
		Single Parent	Coupled Parent
Employment status (%)[a, b, c]			
Currently employed	75.2	77.0	85.5
Currently unemployed	6.6	4.9	2.5
Not in the labor force	18.3	18.1	12.0
Currently employed and enrolled in school[a]	6.4	8.7	7.9
Average number of workers in family[a, b]	1.4	1.2	1.8

SOURCE: ACS-PUMS five-year file, 2016–2020.

[a] Denotes significant difference between veteran and nonveteran single parents at the < 0.01 level.

[b] Denotes significant difference between veteran single parents and veteran coupled parents at the < 0.01 level.

[c] After adjusting for age, race, gender, and educational attainment, nonveteran single parents were more likely to be employed than veteran single parents.

Median Household Income

There were significant differences in median household incomes of veteran single parents by race and ethnicity and gender. Table A.2 provides financial security data by race and ethnicity: The median household income of Black, non-Hispanic veteran single parents was about $10,000 less than the median of any other racial and ethnic subset of the veteran single parent sample. Table A.8 provides financial security data by gender: The median household income for veteran single mothers was $12,000 less than that of their male counterparts of the same race. Table A.14 provides intersectional financial security data: Among veteran single parents, Black mothers reported the lowest median household income ($47,000), and White fathers reported the highest ($67,000)—a difference of $20,000.

Food Insecurity

Our analysis of race, ethnicity, and gender also suggests that some veteran single parents face greater food insecurity than others. Table A.2 provides financial security data by race and ethnicity: A higher percentage of Black (24.7 percent) and Hispanic (19.4 percent) veteran single parents reported receiving SNAP benefits in the past year compared with White (15.6 percent) and Other Race (16.9 percent) veteran single parents. Additionally, 21.2 percent of Hispanic veteran single parents reported using a food pantry in the past 30 days compared with only 6.6 percent of Black veteran single parents, 7.8 percent of White veteran single parents, and 7.7 percent of Other Race veteran single parents. Table A.14 provides intersectional food security data. Of note, 42.9 percent of women who identified as Other Race (i.e., Indian, Alaskan Native, Asian, Native Hawaiian, Other Pacific Islander, or two or more races) reported the highest rates of households "living in a low food security." This is in stark contrast to the veteran single parents in other subgroups, who reported rates that ranged between 12.3 percent and 21.9 percent. Future research should investigate the vulnerability of this veteran group and their families around food security. In addition, 34.4 percent of Other Race (Indian, Alaskan Native, Asian, Native Hawaiian, Other Pacific Islander, or two or more races) mothers also reported that their children received free or reduced-price lunch in the past 30 days, second only to Black men (28.4 percent).

Housing

Table A.9 provides housing data by gender: Veteran single mothers were more likely to spend 50 percent or more of their income on housing than veteran single fathers (20.1 percent versus 12.1 percent). Table A.15 provides intersectional housing data: 22.7 percent of Black veteran single mothers reported spending over half of their income on housing, second only to Hispanic veteran single mothers (25.1 percent).

Education and Employment

Table A.13 provides intersectional demographic data: Black and Hispanic veteran single mothers were more likely than other intersectional groups to be enrolled in higher education (24.1 percent and 20.1 percent, respectively, compared with a range of 6.7–17.8 percent across other groups).

Table A.10 provides employment data by gender: 12.6 percent of veteran single mothers reported being both currently employed and enrolled in school compared with only 5.8 percent of veteran single fathers. Among veteran single mothers, a greater proportion of Black and Hispanic veteran single mothers reported simultaneous employment and schooling than their White and Other Race counterparts. Table A.16 provides this intersectional employment data: Black veteran single mothers were the most likely to report being both employed and enrolled in school (17.3 percent), followed by Hispanic veteran single mothers (13.1 percent); rates for other intersectional groups range between 4.5–10.7 percent.

Summary: Financial Well-Being

In general, financial indicators followed our original hypothesis: Veteran single parents had greater financial security than nonveteran single parents but less than veteran coupled parents. Looking at race and gender within veteran single parents illustrated that veteran single mothers of color faced greater financial insecurity than their White and male counterparts. Male single parents (regardless of marital status or veteran status) typically reported greater financial well-being. Such findings follow existing research that suggests men often have greater levels of support for raising children than mothers. Fathers in a couple often do less child care and domestic work than the mothers in a couple (Horne et al., 2018), and single fathers are also more likely to be living with another adult, which could provide fathers greater flexibility and time to pursue paid labor (Livingston, 2013).

Interestingly, we found that veteran single mothers were more likely than their male counterparts to be pursuing higher education and more likely to be currently employed while enrolled in school. These differences might be driven by the fact that women feel they need higher education to make comparable wages with their male counterparts. Other studies have found that single mothers are enrolled in higher education programs at elevated rates (compared with single fathers), but these studies do not investigate the veteran status of these women (Gault, Milli, and Cruse, 2018). It might be that veteran benefits are driving this high enrollment: Educational benefits provided to veteran single mothers increases the ability of these individuals to pursue an expensive degree and improve their earning potential. However, it likely adds considerably to their already busy schedules, putting pressure on their caring responsibilities and careers.

Finally, specific financial indicators, including household income and food insecurity, showed varying levels of insecurity across race, ethnicity, and gender identities. Veteran mothers who identified as Indian, Alaskan Native, Asian, Native Hawaiian, Other Pacific

Islander, or two or more races showed high rates of food insecurity compared with other groups. Existing literature cannot shed light on why this might be, but future research should investigate.

CHAPTER 4

Mental and Physical Health and Well-Being of Veteran Single Parents

Turning next to mental and physical health and well-being, we saw clear differences between veteran single parents, nonveteran single parents, and veteran coupled parents. It is important to note that, again, these results are unadjusted for age, gender, race, and educational attainment. However, we highlight results that did change when adjusted in the tables below. We also examine the interactions between race and gender and these measures in the next section to understand whether demographic factors are associated with different outcomes.

In general, veteran single parents reported lower mental health than other groups. As outlined in Table 4.1, veteran single parents reported the greatest number of days in which their mental health was "not good" in the past month compared with nonveteran single parents and veteran coupled parents (6.0 days versus 5.8 and 4.0, respectively). Veteran single parents also reported the greatest number of days in which their physical health was "not good" in the past month compared with nonveteran single parents and veteran coupled parents (4.4 days versus 3.4 and 3.2, respectively). However, 54.0 percent of veteran single parents reported "excellent or very good" general health compared with 48.8 percent of their nonveteran counterparts and 60.5 percent of veteran coupled parents. These findings follow our hypothesis that veteran coupled parents would report greater physical and mental health.

However, differences between veteran single parents and nonveteran single parents who reported on general health are harder to unpack. Although veteran single parents reported a greater number of "poor physical or mental health" days than nonveteran single parents, a greater proportion of veteran single parents reported "excellent or very good" health than nonveteran single parents. Further qualitative research could start to unpack this discrepancy across these standard questions.

Access to health care is outlined in Table 4.2. In keeping with our hypotheses, veteran single parents report less access to health care than veteran coupled parents: 12.8 percent of veteran single parents reported no health care coverage, and only 5.3 percent of veteran coupled parents reported no health care coverage. However, veteran single parents are in a better position than nonveteran single parents: 20.7 percent of nonveteran single parents reported no health care coverage. In addition, 16.3 percent of veteran single parents reported being unable to see a doctor in the past year because of cost compared with only 8.0 percent

TABLE 4.1

Mental and Physical Health Self Ratings

Demographic Characteristic	Nonveteran Single Parent	Veteran	
		Single Parent	Coupled Parent
Mean number of days in the past 30 days with each given health state			
Mental health not good[b]	5.8	6.0	4.0
Physical health not good[a, b]	3.4	4.4	3.2
Poor physical or mental health[a, b]	4.8	5.6	4.7
General health status (%)[a, b, c]			
Excellent or very good	48.8	54.0	60.5
Good	34.1	30.2	28.7
Fair or poor	17.1	15.7	10.9

SOURCE: BRFSS, five-year data, 2016–2020.

[a] Denotes significant difference between veteran and nonveteran single parents at the < 0.01 level.

[b] Denotes significant difference between veteran single parents and veteran coupled parents at the < 0.01 level.

[c] After adjusting for age, race, gender, and educational attainment, the difference between veteran and nonveteran single parents became insignificant for "fair or poor" health reporting.

TABLE 4.2

Access to Health Care

Demographic Characteristic	Nonveteran Single Parent	Veteran	
		Single Parent	Coupled Parent
No health care coverage (%)[a, b]	20.7	12.8	5.3
No personal doctor (%)[b]	33.4	33.5	24.4
No routine checkup in last year (%)[a, b]	32.6	28.1	24.8
Could not see doctor in last year because of cost (%)[a, b, c]	19.8	16.3	8.0

SOURCE: BRFSS, five-year data, 2016–2020.

[a] Denotes significant difference between veteran and nonveteran single parents at the < 0.01 level.

[b] Denotes significant difference between veteran single parents and veteran coupled parents at the < 0.01 level.

[c] After adjusting for age, race, gender, and educational attainment, the difference between veteran and nonveteran single parents became insignificant.

of veteran coupled parents. Again, nonveteran single parents reported the most difficulty: 19.8 percent reported being unable to see a doctor in the past year because of cost.

Considering Gender, Race, and Ethnicity in Health and Well-Being Outcomes

We examined these health and well-being outcomes data across gender, race, and ethnic identity. The full tables can be found in the appendix. Here we outline the most prominent intersectional differences across these health and well-being measures.

Mental and Physical Health

Table A.11 provides mental and physical health self-ratings data by gender: Veteran single mothers reported 7.1 days out of the past month in which their mental health was not good compared with 5.6 days reported by veteran single fathers.

Table A.17 provides intersectional mental and physical health self-ratings data: Hispanic single mothers reported the highest number of days out of the past month (8.6 days) in which their mental health was not good; the days reported by other intersectional groups ranged between 4.9–7.5. In addition, 27.1 percent of Hispanic single mothers reported "fair or poor" general health status, in contrast with other intersectional groups in which a range of 13.6–19.7 percent reported "fair or poor" general health.

Access to Health Care

Table A.12 provides health care access data by gender: Veteran single fathers were more likely than their female counterparts to report having "no health care coverage" (13.9 percent versus 9.9 percent), "no personal doctor" (37.5 percent versus 23.1 percent), and "no routine checkup in past year" (30.2 percent versus 22.7 percent). However, a greater proportion of veteran single mothers than veteran single fathers reported not being able to see a doctor in the past year because of cost (19.6 percent versus 15.0 percent).

Table A.18 provides intersectional health care access data: There were two intersectional groups in which the gender differences identified above do not hold. Veteran single fathers were more likely than their female counterparts to report having "no health care coverage" in each race category except for Hispanic. A slightly higher proportion of Hispanic veteran single mothers than Hispanic veteran single fathers reported "no health care coverage" (16.7 percent versus 16.1 percent). In addition, a greater proportion of veteran single mothers than veteran single fathers reported not being able to see a doctor in the past year because of cost in each race category except for Black, non-Hispanic. There is a higher proportion of Black veteran single fathers than Black veteran single mothers who report not being able to see a doctor in the past year because of cost (16.8 percent versus 12.9 percent).

Summary: Physical and Mental Well-Being

In sum, veteran single parents and nonveteran single parents reported poorer health and well-being than veteran coupled parents. Interestingly, veteran single parents reported a greater number of "poor physical or mental health" days than nonveteran single parents, and a greater proportion of veteran single parents reported "excellent or very good" health than nonveteran single parents. One possibility is that this disparity highlights differences in expectations around health between veterans and nonveterans; veteran single parents might be more likely to expect poorer physical health than nonveterans. Both groups reported difficulty accessing health care compared with veteran coupled parents, although nonveteran single parents reported the greatest difficulty.

Looking specifically at veteran single parents across demographic factors revealed that veteran single mothers faced greater strain on their mental health compared with veteran single fathers and coupled parents. Hispanic veteran single mothers reported the greatest number of "not good" mental health days in the past month. Cost was also more likely to be a barrier to health care for veteran single mothers than veteran single fathers, except for Black veteran single parents. These findings follow research that found that single mothers are more likely to struggle with mental health (Jayakody and Stauffer, 2002). Single mothers are also more likely to shift economic resources to their children's health care costs and away from their own in hard economic times (Monheit, Grafova, and Kumar, 2020). These results are also in line with existing research that found that woman veterans are more likely to suffer from posttraumatic stress disorder, anxiety, depression, and suicidal ideation than male veterans (Adams et al., 2021).

However, veteran single fathers were more likely to report no personal doctor and more likely to report no routine checkup in the past year, suggesting that, although cost might be less of an issue, other barriers to care might be at play for veteran single fathers. This finding follows existing research that found that single fathers are also less likely to take their children to routine health screenings than single mothers (Gorman and Braverman, 2008). Our data suggest that barriers to health care providers that single fathers face also extend to their own care, in addition to their children.

CHAPTER 5

The Experience of Veteran Single Parents in Higher Education

The previous chapters provided a broad overview of who veteran single parents are and how they are doing financially, mentally, and physically, relative to nonveterans and veteran coupled parents. Among others, one finding struck us: high rates of enrollment in higher education especially among Black and Hispanic veteran single mothers. This suggests, potentially, that educational benefits provided by the G.I. Bill are a resource that could lift the economic well-being of veteran single parents—potentially to the level of veteran coupled parents. But, given the difficulties single parents face juggling child care and work, we felt we needed more information to understand how veteran single parents were also adding higher education to their busy schedules.

The next section uses data from semistructured interviews with veteran single parents in higher education to investigate barriers and facilitators to their pursuit of higher education. We focused on how policies, such as the G.I. Bill, supported veteran single parents' educational goals while they parented small children. Such policies as the G.I. Bill are designed to support veterans as they transition from service into civilian life, but caring for a child without support from a partner could, theoretically, make it more difficult to use those benefits. However, our analysis of the ACS suggests that veteran single parents are more in need of such support to increase their incomes, access essentials, and gain economic security. Our finding that a high percentage of veteran single mothers of color were enrolled in higher education suggests that single parents might utilize this benefit to improve their circumstances despite difficulties inherent in raising a child or children alone. Our qualitative interviews were designed to understand why veteran single parents enrolled in higher education, what their experience in higher education was like, and any barriers or facilitators they encountered while pursuing a degree.

We conducted 11 semistructured interviews with student veteran single parents. The interview sample consisted of five men and six women who were raising between one and five children and currently attending or attended college in the last five years. The children's ages ranged from infants to teenagers during the time the veteran was enrolled.[1] Those interviewed typically started pursuing higher education a few years after having

---

[1] We did not ask detailed information about children in the interviews to preserve their privacy.

left the military, and one of the interviewees was a nonveteran school administrator whose job is to support student veterans. The interview questions were designed to elicit descriptions of interviewees' experiences, with an eye toward identifying barriers experienced when they tried to pursue higher education. Although the sample was relatively small, we reached saturation with our qualitative data quickly; veterans highlighted the same core factors that facilitated or impeded their pursuit of higher education.

Broadly speaking, the 11 student veteran single parents interviewed had very positive associations with the pursuit of higher education and used words like *passion, interest,* and *love* to describe choosing their field of study. All interviewees described a desire to improve quality of life for themselves and their children through their education and expected it to lead to jobs that were higher paying, more stable, and personally fulfilling. Indeed, some interviewees noted that their desire to obtain a post-secondary degree led them to consider entering the military.

Unfortunately, most of the interviewees faced significant barriers to attaining higher education, despite all being eligible for G.I. Bill benefits, which aim to support veterans interested in attaining education and training. In the interviews, veterans shared their biggest challenges as a student veteran and single parent, as well as existing or potential facilitators that allowed them to overcome those barriers. Veteran single parents also provided specific recommendations to improve access to higher education for future veteran parents. We summarize the key themes voiced by veteran single parents in higher education below.[2]

Child Care

Lack of affordable child care was, by far, the greatest and most frequently mentioned challenge. All 11 interviewees described barriers and challenges with child care. Veterans who are students and single parents have a lot to balance, especially when their children are young (between birth and 3 years old). Child care is both time-consuming and expensive, and student veterans often have neither the time nor the money required for adequate child care.

> My older children can hang out. I'll put a movie on for them while I'm in class. It's the six-month-old who needs my attention. She needs to be changed and talked to, which is difficult to do while taking notes. —Student

> I'm lucky because she's 11 and responsible. She can be home alone for several hours. But if she was younger, I'd be forced to pay for child care and it would be an extreme challenge. —Student

These veterans often find themselves in a catch-22: If they do not spend money on child care, they spend more time taking care of their children and their learning suffers. If they do

---

[2] Note that quotes may be paraphrased for brevity.

spend money on child care, they spend more time working to pay for that child care and their learning still suffers. The most common solution among interviewees was family support.

> If it wasn't for my family, I'd be struggling right now. Child care is really, really expensive. —Student

Without family support, these veterans have few options. Lack of affordable child care for this vulnerable population of veterans can have devastating consequences, not only for parents who must make enormous sacrifices but also for children who inherit the consequences of those sacrifices.

> I was at the brink. If I didn't have family, I would have easily become homeless at that point. But because I had people, I was able to hang on for a little bit. —Student

> I ended up living on the streets with a baby and an 11-year-old. My friend let me stay with her until I finish school but did not want my kids in the house. So my older daughter is with her dad. And my baby, I placed her in adoption. —Student

> I really don't get to see my daughter much. I go to class from 9 a.m. to 2 p.m., and then I go to work from 2 p.m. to 8:30 p.m., Monday through Friday. But if I didn't have help from family, I probably wouldn't be able to do it, or I wouldn't be able to work. —Student

Veterans Resource Centers

Veterans Resource Centers (VRCs) and veterans' representatives make an enormous difference for student veterans with limited personal and family resources. VRCs aim to assist veteran students and their families with needs related to their educational benefits and VA. VRCs can provide different services and have different types of physical locations, but, in general, they provide support for accessing VA educational benefits (e.g., G.I. Bill), including helping veterans fill out forms and navigate bureaucracy, access community resources, and find employment opportunities in or through VA. VRCs can provide quiet spaces for studying or rooms for meetings or clubs and just generally provide space for veterans to connect with each other. VRCs might be staffed by professional administrators or veterans.

These supports provided by VA, colleges, and universities can reduce adverse consequences by assisting veterans who might not have social and financial safety nets. Student veteran single parents often do not have time to fully understand their benefits or know where to ask for help, especially when they do not have family support. VRCs and representatives can make existing resources more accessible and thus prevent the most-vulnerable veterans from slipping through the cracks. However, the existence and robustness of these VRCs and representatives are inconsistent across colleges and universities, leading to highly variable experiences and outcomes.

There's no time to read through the pamphlets. . . . I didn't have time to investigate. I was being charged by the hour for my kid to be watched. There wasn't anyone saying, "If you need help, here are your options." —Student

I will not go to any school that doesn't have a vet center. Not anymore. It's helped me so much. . . . They had an advisor walking me through the process. He's like, "Here's a checklist of what you need to get me. Do this, do that." It worked out pretty well. —Student

To be honest, I don't really know how the G.I. Bill works. There really should be a place where you could call and directly talk to someone. The information is not as accessible as people would like it to be. —Student

Our veterans center's family lounge has toys and coloring books and all that kind of stuff. Having that space where your kid can be playing, not just stuck to a tablet, while you study. It is a really big thing. —Student

G.I. Bill Requirements

The G.I. Bill makes higher education possible for many veterans who would not have access otherwise. The G.I. Bill was signed into law by President Franklin D. Roosevelt on June 22, 1944, and provided World War II veterans with funds for college education, unemployment insurance, and housing ("Servicemen's Readjustment Act [1944]," undated). Since 1944, the G.I. Bill has evolved. The Post-9/11 G.I. Bill, in particular, provided veterans who joined the military after September 11, 2001, with different support than previous iterations. Briefly, veterans who (1) served at least 90 days on active duty (either all at once or with breaks in service) on or after September 11, 2001; (2) received a Purple Heart on or after September 11, 2001, and were honorably discharged after any amount of service; or (3) served for at least 30 continuous days (all at once, without a break in service) on or after September 11, 2001, and were honorably discharged with a service-connected disability qualify for these supports. The bill provides funding for tuition and fees, housing while enrolled in higher education, books and supplies, and moving costs to attend school (VA, undated-a).

However, qualitative interview data suggest that G.I. Bill benefits have requirements that often do not account for the time constraints and financial realities of single parents. As examples, G.I. Bill beneficiaries must attend at least one in-person class to be eligible for their full housing allowance, they are expected to pay back tuition for any courses from which they withdraw, and the housing allowance they receive is prorated to the number of credits for which they are currently enrolled.

Three out of the 11 interviewees identified the in-person class requirement as a challenge. Attending an in-person class requires single parents to find and pay for local housing, transportation, and child care. Although the G.I. Bill does allow for students to take online-only classes, this option offers a housing allowance that is only half the average military housing allowance in the country. This might be much lower than the average rent in the area in which veteran single parents live, making in-person classes the only financially viable option for veteran single parents.

Consequently, most veterans sign up to attend one class in person to receive their full housing benefit based on the average cost of housing in their zip code. Despite higher housing allowances, veteran single parents still struggle financially. Lower-cost housing is generally found farther away from school campuses, but living farther away from campus means that transportation and time costs associated with attending in-person class are higher. In these situations, child care becomes a necessity, especially for parents of younger children. If friends or family cannot provide free child care, then the cost burden of child care falls entirely on the student. The increase in the housing allowance provided by taking at least one in-person class often makes this trade-off worth it from a financial perspective, but the added stress and financial strain are significant for veteran single parents.

> In-person class requires them to leave their house twice a week for an hour and a half, plus travel time. So with parents, especially single parents, they have to find someone to watch their child. That's a big issue. —Administrator

> The requirement to have one sit-in class at school while having young kids, that was really hard for me. Especially when your kids get sick and bring down the whole house. And if you have sick kids, there are zero options for child care. —Student

The requirement to pay tuition back for any class from which students withdraw also poses a financial barrier. Many interviewees described a lack of social and financial safety net while pursuing higher education, meaning any unforeseen event could have an outsized impact. This was acutely relevant when utilizing G.I. Bill benefits. For example, if a single parent missed classes to care for sick children during a particularly bad flu season, they might be forced to withdraw from a class or two. In doing so, however, they are required to pay back the tuition for that class, further burdening an already burdened single parent.

> Because of [the coronavirus disease 2019], I'm parenting my kids, so I withdrew. I made a choice to parent my kids better, but I had to pay back the VA because I didn't get the grades. —Student

Ten out of the 11 interviewees mentioned barriers and challenges to either housing or living with family. The G.I. Bill provides a housing allowance for students. This allowance is based on the cost of living where the veteran's university resides. Consequently, a veteran going to the University of California, Berkeley, is given over $3,000 a month during the school year for housing compared with a veteran attending University of California, Merced, who would receive $1,700 a month (VA, undated-b). Moreover, if a student decides to attend remotely, they only receive half of the average housing allowance for the country, or $938.50 as of 2023 (VA, undated-c).

The housing allowance is helpful but often not enough, especially for single parents. It is also directly tied to the number of credits that a student is taking, so a single parent whose life constraints require part-time student status is further disadvantaged by a reduced housing allowance. Moreover, students do not receive allowance during summer, winter, and spring breaks; this inconsistent income can be especially prohibitive for single parents.

> Because I'm a student parent, I only take half time classes. My housing allowance is pro-rated to the amount of credits I'm taking. —Student

> Unfortunately, I think the VA means for the housing allowance to be supplemental, which then pushes the individual into having to work. But if you have a child, you work to pay daycare and then you still don't have any money left. . . . One veteran intended to use his benefits to support his children. He signed up for classes and everything, and then found out that he didn't get paid until the end of each month after classes started, and he withdrew because he couldn't wait that long. He had to go to work. —Administrator

> You cannot live on the basic allowance for housing. You have to work. With children, it's even worse. If I didn't have my disability benefits, I would not have been able to afford child care. Last year, I paid $19,000 for daycare for two children, so it's a lot. My disability benefit was $39,000 for the year. —Student

The data described above suggest that there are significant gaps in the availability of educational benefits for veteran single parents. As we discuss in the next chapter, greater attention to the unique needs of veteran single parents could increase access to G.I. Bill benefits and address inequalities between veteran single parents and veteran coupled parents.

CHAPTER 6

Conclusions and Recommendations

Our investigation of the mental, physical, and financial well-being of veteran parents revealed several key findings. Veteran single parents are demographically different, on average, from veteran coupled parents and nonveteran single parents. Veteran single parents are more likely to be female and more likely to identify as part of a marginalized racial or ethnic group compared with veteran coupled parents. However, because the veteran population is predominantly male, about half of veteran single parents are fathers.

Veteran single parents face greater financial insecurity than veteran coupled parents but have greater financial security than nonveteran single parents. Individually, veteran single parents make about $18,000 less per year than a veteran coupled parent, and their median household income is $50,000 less than that of a veteran coupled parent. However, nonveteran single parents make less than veteran single parents, individually (median of $18,000 less) and at the household level (median of $16,000 less).

Veteran single parents and nonveteran single parents are much more likely to live with food insecurity than veteran coupled parents (17.3 percent versus 4.4 percent). However, veteran single parents are less likely to access state-funded support for people experiencing food insecurity, such as SNAP. These findings follow research that suggests that veterans are less likely to take advantage of such programs as SNAP despite being food insecure (Hall, 2021; Pooler et al., 2021; Dubowitz, 2021). Our analysis suggests that this pattern extends, perhaps more acutely, to vulnerable veteran single parent families.

Veteran single parents are almost three times more likely than veteran coupled parents to spend more than 50 percent of their income on housing (15.5 percent versus 5.5 percent). Many veteran single parents are living in their parents' home (16.6 percent); very few veteran coupled parents do so (1.8 percent). However, across these metrics, nonveteran single parents face greater financial and housing instability.

Veteran single parents and nonveteran single parents reported poorer health and well-being than veteran coupled parents and lower access to health care services than veteran coupled parents. Looking at variation by gender, veteran single mothers reported higher rates of mental health issues and greater cost barriers to health care, while veteran single fathers reported lower levels of access to health insurance and less use of health care. Looking at intersecting gender and race identities, however, Hispanic veteran single mothers are more likely to struggle with mental health, and cost was a barrier to health care for veteran single mothers more often than to veteran single fathers (except for Black veteran single parents). Such differences could be caused or compounded by financial strain in these families.

All these findings follow a central theme: Being in a partnership and being a veteran is correlated with greater financial, mental, and physical well-being and greater access to health care services. Nonveteran single parents face difficult odds and struggle to gain financial security, although their health indicators are similar to their veteran parent counterparts. It seems likely that access to services tailored to support former service members could dampen any financial, physical, or mental health strains of raising a child without the support of the other parent of that child. However, these benefits do not close the gap between veteran coupled parents and veteran single parents. Understanding what is driving these persistent differences could help policymakers better target policies and programs to veteran single parents.

Importantly, demographic differences between veteran coupled parents and veteran single parents could drive some of these results: Veteran coupled parents are more likely to be older and male than veteran single parents and nonveteran single parents, both characteristics correlated with higher income and financial stability (Bishu and Alkadry, 2017; Ozhamaratli, Kitov, and Barucca, 2022). Existing literature also suggests that single fathers might have greater family and other supports as they raise children than single mothers (Livingston, 2013). As research on this group moves forward, policymakers should examine the unique needs of veteran single parents whatever the driving factor behind these differences is.

One example of a policy that should help close the gap between veteran coupled parents and veteran single parents, but does not always succeed, is the G.I. Bill. Veteran parents are using their G.I. Bill benefits. Indeed, a higher percentage of veteran single parents reported being enrolled in school than veteran coupled parents (13.1 percent versus 10.7 percent). Black and Hispanic veteran single mothers reported the highest rates of school enrollment (24.1 percent and 20.1 percent, respectively). Veteran single mothers are also more likely than veteran single fathers to be enrolled in school while simultaneously employed (12.6 percent versus 5.8 percent).

However, qualitative interviews with veteran single parents pursuing higher education revealed significant barriers to using G.I. Bill benefits. Almost all interviewees discussed the difficulty of affording child care, working, and managing academic workload simultaneously. Specific aspects of the G.I. Bill were also burdensome for veteran single parents, particularly requirements to attend one class in person to receive full housing benefits.

Recommendations

To reach parity with veteran coupled parents, veteran single parents need greater financial support when transitioning out of the military and into civilian jobs or education. Without support from another parent, veteran single parents likely have even greater demands on their time (full-time child-rearing) and resources (only one income) than veteran coupled parents. The fact that parents from ethnic and racial minority groups and woman veteran single parents face greater hardship than their White and male counterparts after leaving the military suggests that broader systemic inequalities in the United States also negatively affect veterans. Policies designed to support veteran single parents can improve equity in services, support, and outcomes for all veterans. Our recommendations are as follows:

- **Target transition services for veteran single parents as a unique group.** Veteran single parents might need additional guidance on career paths that allow them to balance family and career, affordable child care options, and information about how to apply for benefits, such as SNAP and other financial resources, as they transition out of the service. Although women are more likely to be single mothers than men are to be single fathers, half of all veteran single parents are men, so these efforts should be gender-inclusive and welcoming to single fathers. Research on nonveteran parents suggest that single fathers and fathers, more generally, feel alienated from professional services (e.g., education, health care) when seeking support for their children (Coles, 2015). Our veteran interviewees expressed similar barriers to support.
- **Provide federal financial support for child care for veterans.** Although there are many benefits offered to veterans who care for others (e.g., VA Dependent Parent Program) or family members of veterans (e.g., surviving spouse and child benefits), a limited number of programs and policies support veterans who are parents. Interestingly, there is a program that helps VA employees who are parents that earn below a certain income threshold for child care (VA Child Care Subsidy Program) but no similar program that specifically helps veterans with young children. Nongovernmental organizations like the Foundation for Women Warriors attempt to support woman veterans who need child care but are unable to extend these services to all veterans who need them. The demand for services from the Foundation for Women Warriors underlines the need for greater access to such services provided, ideally, by the VA and federal government.
- **Provide support for single parents in higher education.** We found that a relatively high percentage of the most financially insecure families headed by veteran single parents were enrolled in higher education. These statistics suggest a commitment among veteran single parents to improve their future income levels and career trajectories to benefit themselves and their families. However, juggling school and being a full-time parent presents high barriers to completing education and fully using G.I. Bill benefits guaranteed to veterans. Key components of the G.I. Bill make completing a degree difficult for veteran single parents. By adjusting in-person requirements, waiving withdrawal penalties, and increasing the affordability of part-time degree participation, single parents could benefit from higher education as much as veteran coupled parents and veterans without children do (see Yi and Smucker [2024] for a deeper dive on this topic).
- **Provide mental health care for veteran single mothers.** Veteran single mothers reported higher rates of poor mental health than their male counterparts. Our analysis of survey data cannot tell us why this might be. However, given the higher rates of financial insecurity among women (especially women from minority ethnic and racial backgrounds) in our study, higher rates of financial insecurity might be related to poorer

mental health outcomes for women. Other research also finds that woman veterans are more likely to have experienced military sexual trauma, depression, anxiety, and other common mental health disorders, which could contribute to this difference (Adams et al., 2021). Ensuring that single mothers have access to mental health support could help not only mothers but also their children.

- **Encourage single fathers to seek out primary care.** Veteran single fathers reported lower rates of health care seeking than did single mothers. These findings follow research that suggests single fathers are less likely to seek out health and behavioral health services for their children (Coles, 2015). Although our data cannot determine exactly why this is, it might be that fathers are less likely than mothers to engage in help seeking. Existing research finds that men are less likely to engage in help-seeking behaviors than women, especially for mental health concerns (Nam et al., 2010), and fathers also struggle to engage support resources (Ghaleiha et al., 2022). Ensuring that veteran single fathers are encouraged to access primary care could improve their long-term outcomes and ability to care for their children.

Future Research

This analysis raises many questions about the experience of veteran single parents. One central question is: What is driving differences in financial well-being and physical and mental health among veteran single parents, veteran coupled parents, and nonveteran single parents? Although the present analysis provided some explanations based on existing research, our approach cannot determine whether such demographic characteristics as age and gender or military experience are driving differences among groups. Going forward, we hope to develop analyses that include the same or similar data but use more-advanced statistical analyses to isolate outcomes most associated with veteran and marital status.

Our intersectional analysis highlighted the importance of drilling down into subgroups to understand the unique issues facing veteran parents. We found significant differences in reported food insecurity among mothers who identified as Other Race (Indian, Alaska Native, Asian, Native Hawaiian, Other Pacific Islander, or two or more races); over one-third reported that their children received free or reduced-price lunches in the last 30 days. We also found that Hispanic single mothers were struggling with mental health more than other groups and that Black single fathers were more likely to report issues accessing health care than other groups. Future research could continue to focus on these groups to identify their unique experiences and policies that would better meet their needs.

Finally, future research should unpack how different child custody or child support arrangements affect veteran single parents. It seems likely that certain custody arrangements and child support levels could influence the financial pressure faced by veteran single parents. Moreover, veterans might have unique child custody arrangements if they were single parents prior to or during their military career. Because about 5 percent of active-duty service members identify as a single parent, the experience of single parenthood in the military and as a veteran could involve compounding issues, especially if children were sent to live with another relative while the parent deployed (Military OneSource, undated). Future surveys or qualitative work could better capture how child care arrangements mediate the outcomes documented in this report.

Limitations

Our analysis is limited in several ways. First, we did not adjust for demographic characteristics in our analysis. This means that the differences we saw between parents and veterans could be highly correlated with other factors that we did not account for. As we mentioned previously, we viewed this analysis as a first step toward understanding the unique circumstances that drive veteran single parents' experiences and account for differences between their well-being and those of veteran coupled parents and nonveteran single parents.

Another limitation is our sample. Although the ACS and BRFSS provide one of the most representative samples of veterans, our analysis focused on averages from a broad period (2016–2021), which could mask more-subtle variation in results in specific years. We were also limited by information collected by the ACS and BRFSS. We did not know, for example, whether individuals receive or pay child support while raising children on their own. We also did not know whether children were born before the person became a veteran or after. Having children while in the military or before military service has unique impacts on children, especially children with single parents (e.g., when a parent deploys). Qualitative data could get closer to unpacking these relationships. We also did not compare how the age of the child mediated parent outcomes, which limited our ability to understand differences in outcomes across newer and more-established parents.

Finally, we captured only qualitative data from a narrow group of veterans: veteran single parents who are or were previously enrolled in higher education. As a result, the qualitative component has limited validity outside that narrow group. However, understanding barriers veteran single parents face when trying to use benefits associated with military service sheds light on reasons why veteran single parents do not use their higher education benefits. As many of our interviewees attested, they often relied on outside help from family or charity to get through their education while raising children on their own. We can infer that there are many veteran single parents who do not have access to such resources and, consequently, never enroll in school. Future research should engage in more qualitative data collection across a broader range of veteran single parents.

Intersectional Analysis: Race and Gender

This appendix provides Tables A.1 through A.18 from our analysis of race and gender across veteran single parents. Note that we do not provide an intersectional analysis of the entire sample of parents, but we did perform this analysis and could provide further information if requested.

TABLE A.1

Racial and Ethnic Differences in Demographic Characteristics Across Veteran Single Parents

Demographic Characteristic	Black, Non-Hispanic (%) (n = 70,770)	White, Non-Hispanic (%) (n = 165,521)	Hispanic (%) (n = 37,916)	Other (%) (n = 20,470)
Age[a]				
18–29 years	13.8	8.1	12.8	11.3
30–39 years	36.6	32.8	42.9	40.6
40–49 years	33.3	39.2	32.8	34.5
50–59 years	16.4	19.8	11.4	13.6
Sex[a]				
Female	61.5	34.1	45.3	43.1
Male	38.5	65.9	64.7	56.9
Educational attainment[a]				
Less than high school	3.1	1.9	5.5	2.5
High school graduate or GED	18.6	21.4	15.7	16.1
Some college with no degree	47.9	47.2	53.7	46.9
Bachelor's degree or higher	30.4	29.5	25.1	34.6
Enrolled in higher education[a]	18.8	9.6	17.2	14.2
Average number of children	1.5	1.5	1.7	1.6

SOURCE: ACS-PUMS, five-year file, 2016–2020.

[a] Denotes significant differences by race and ethnicity within veterans at the < 0.01 level.

TABLE A.2

Racial and Ethnic Differences in Financial Security Across Veteran Single Parents

Demographic Characteristic	Black, Non-Hispanic	White, Non-Hispanic	Hispanic	Other
Median personal income[a]	$35,000	$45,000	$42,000	$39,400
Median household income[a]	$49,500	$62,380	$58,600	$59,000
Percentage receiving the following forms of assistance				
Self-employment income[a]	3.6	5.5	3.3	6.1
SSI	2.7	2.4	2.1	2.3
Public assistance income	3.2	2.6	3.0	4.0
Retirement income	13.2	13.4	12.1	11.2
SNAP benefits in last year[a]	24.7	15.6	19.4	16.9
No health insurance[a]	4.4	6.0	4.9	9.7
Food security (%)				
Living in a low food security household	20.3	15.2	15.0	22.8
Living in a very low food security household	6.2	5.1	4.8	5.8
Receipt of free/reduced-price lunch in last 30 days	24.7	19.2	17.4	15.5
Use of food pantry in last 30 days	6.6	7.8	21.2	7.7

SOURCE: ACS-PUMS, five-year file, 2016–2020; CPS-FSS, pooled 2016–2020.

[a] Denotes significant differences by race and ethnicity within veterans at the < 0.01 level.

TABLE A.3

Racial and Ethnic Differences in Housing Across Veteran Single Parents

Demographic Characteristic	Black, Non-Hispanic (%)	White, Non-Hispanic (%)	Hispanic (%)	Other (%)
Homeownership[a]				
Home owned with mortgage	34.0	48.3	40.9	38.8
Home owned free and clear	9.0	14.0	13.4	13.9
Home rented	57.0	37.7	45.7	47.3
Subfamily household				
Primary household	80.1	81.5	78.8	77.2
Living in parent household	16.5	16.2	17.5	18.9
Living in another household	3.3	2.3	3.7	3.9
Percentage of income spent on housing costs[a]				
< 10%	7.0	12.1	8.9	11.8

Table A.3—Continued

Demographic Characteristic	Black, Non-Hispanic (%)	White, Non-Hispanic (%)	Hispanic (%)	Other (%)
10–19.9%	20.1	29.5	26.7	21.9
20–29.9%	23.2	25.2	20.0	20.1
30–39.9%	16.6	12.2	15.0	15.6
40–49.9%	9.0	6.2	8.1	8.6
> 50%	20.9	12.2	18.8	18.4

SOURCE: ACS-PUMS, five-year file, 2016–2020.
[a] Denotes significant differences by race and ethnicity within veterans at the < 0.01 level.

TABLE A.4
Racial and Ethnic Differences in Employment Across Veteran Single Parents

Demographic Characteristic	Black, Non-Hispanic	White, Non-Hispanic	Hispanic	Other
Employment status (%)				
Currently employed	74.4	78.3	76.9	76.1
Currently unemployed	5.7	4.5	4.6	5.8
Not in the labor force	19.9	17.2	18.5	18.2
Currently employed and enrolled in school[a]	13.2	6.1	11.8	9.0
Average number of workers in family	1.2	1.2	1.3	1.3

SOURCE: ACS-PUMS, five-year file, 2016–2020.
[a] Denotes significant differences by race and ethnicity within veterans at the < 0.01 level.

TABLE A.5
Racial and Ethnic Differences in Mental and Physical Health Self Ratings Across Veteran Single Parents

Demographic Characteristic	Black, Non-Hispanic	White, Non-Hispanic	Hispanic	Other
Mean number of days in the last 30 days with each given health state				
Mental health not good[a]	5.3	6.0	6.1	7.3
Physical health not good	4.2	4.3	4.5	4.9
Poor physical or mental health	5.8	5.3	6.7	5.5
General health status (%)				
Excellent or very good	52.9	56.5	52.2	47.1
Good	31.8	29.5	28.4	34.2
Fair or poor	15.4	14.0	19.4	18.7

Table A.5—Continued

Demographic Characteristic	Black, Non-Hispanic	White, Non-Hispanic	Hispanic	Other

SOURCE: BRFSS, pooled 2016–2020.

[a] Denotes significant differences by race and ethnicity within veterans at the < 0.01 level.

TABLE A.6

Racial and Ethnic Differences in Access to Health Care Across Veteran Single Parents

Demographic Characteristic	Black, Non-Hispanic (%)	White, Non-Hispanic (%)	Hispanic (%)	Other (%)
No health care coverage	13.5	11.4	16.3	12.0
No personal doctor[a]	27.7	34.0	39.3	33.6
No routine checkup in last year[a]	19.9	32.4	26.7	28.1
Could not see doctor in last year because of cost	15.3	15.8	17.6	18.5

SOURCE: BRFSS, pooled 2016–2020.

[a] Denotes significant differences by race and ethnicity within veterans at the < 0.01 level.

TABLE A.7

Gender Differences in Demographic Characteristics Across Veteran Single Parents

Demographic Characteristic	Women (%) (n = 126,029)	Men (%) (n = 168,648)
Age[a]		
18–29 years	13.6	7.9
30–39 years	41.6	31.1
40–49 years	34.0	38.6
50–59 years	10.9	22.4
Race and ethnicity[a]		
Black, non-Hispanic	34.6	16.1
White, non-Hispanic	44.8	64.7
Asian, non-Hispanic	1.6	1.4
Native Hawaiian or Pacific Islander, non-Hispanic	0.3	0.3
American Indian or Alaskan Native, non-Hispanic	0.8	1.3
Two or more races, non-Hispanic	4.1	3.5
Other, non-Hispanic	0.2	0.3

Table A.7—Continued

Demographic Characteristic	Women (%) (n = 126,029)	Men (%) (n = 168,648)
Hispanic	13.6	12.3
Educational attainment[a]		
Less than high school	1.8	3.4
High school graduate or GED	13.0	24.6
Some college with no degree	49.1	47.5
Bachelor's degree or higher	36.2	24.5
Enrolled in higher education[a]	19.1	8.6
Average number of children[a]	1.6	1.5

SOURCE: ACS-PUMS, five-year file, 2016–2020.

[a] Denotes significant differences by race and ethnicity within veterans at the < 0.01 level.

TABLE A.8
Gender Differences in Financial Security Across Veteran Single Parents

Demographic Characteristic	Women	Men
Median personal income[a]	$36,200	$47,000
Median household income[a]	$51,000	$63,400
Percentage receiving the following forms of assistance		
Self-employment income[a]	3.8	5.6
SSI[a]	1.9	2.8
Public assistance income[a]	3.6	2.3
Retirement income	13.1	13.0
SNAP benefits in last year[a]	23.0	14.9
No health insurance[a]	4.6	6.6
Food security (%)		
Living in a low food security household[a]	23.3	13.6
Living in a very low food security household[a]	9.5	2.7
Receipt of free/reduced-price lunch in last 30 days	24.8	16.8
Use of food pantry in last 30 days[a]	13.0	5.4

SOURCE: ACS-PUMS, five-year file, 2016–2020; CPS-FSS pooled 2016–2020.

[a] Denotes significant differences by race and ethnicity within veterans at the < 0.01 level.

TABLE A.9

Gender Differences in Housing Across Veteran Single Parents

Demographic Characteristic	Women (%)	Men (%)
Homeownership[a]		
Home owned with mortgage	40.7	45.2
Home owned free and clear	10.5	14.4
Home rented	48.8	40.4
Subfamily household		
Primary household	81.0	80.2
Living in parent household	16.0	17.1
Living in another household	3.0	2.7
Percentage of income spent on housing costs[a]		
< 10%	8.2	12.1
10–19.9%	20.9	30.5
20–29.9%	22.9	24.3
30–39.9%	15.9	12.3
40–49.9%	8.7	6.3
> 50%	20.1	12.1

SOURCE: ACS-PUMS, five-year file, 2016–2020.

[a] Denotes significant differences by race and ethnicity within veterans at the < 0.01 level.

TABLE A.10

Gender Differences in Employment Across Veteran Single Parents

Demographic Characteristic	Women	Men
Employment status (%)[a]		
Currently employed	74.6	78.9
Currently unemployed	4.7	5.1
Not in the labor force	20.8	16.0
Currently employed and enrolled in school[a]	12.6	5.8
Average number of workers in family	1.2	1.2

SOURCE: ACS-PUMS, five-year file, 2016–2020.

[a] Denotes significant differences by race and ethnicity within veterans at the < 0.01 level.

TABLE A.11

Gender Differences in Mental and Physical Health Self Ratings Across Veteran Single Parents

Demographic Characteristic	Women	Men
Mean number of days in the last 30 days with each given health state		
Mental health not good[a]	7.1	5.6
Physical health not good	4.6	4.3
Poor physical or mental health	5.7	5.6
General health status (%)		
Excellent or very good	50.4	55.4
Good	32.8	29.2
Fair or poor	16.7	15.3

SOURCE: BRFSS, pooled 2016–2020.

[a] Denotes significant differences by race and ethnicity within veterans at the < 0.01 level.

TABLE A.12

Gender Differences in Access to Health Care Across Veteran Single Parents

Demographic Characteristic	Women (%)	Men (%)
No health care coverage[a]	9.9	13.9
No personal doctor[a]	23.1	37.5
No routine checkup in last year[a]	22.7	30.2
Could not see doctor in last year because of cost	19.6	15.0

SOURCE: BRFSS, pooled 2016–2020.

[a] Denotes significant differences by race and ethnicity within veterans at the < 0.01 level.

TABLE A.13

Racial and Ethnic Differences by Gender in Demographic Characteristics Across Veteran Single Parents

Demographic Characteristic	Black, Non-Hispanic (%)		White, Non-Hispanic (%)		Hispanic (%)		Other (%)	
	Women	Men	Women	Men	Women	Men	Women	Men
Age[a]								
18–29 years	16.1	10.1	11.1	6.6	14.5	11.5	15.2	8.4
30–39 years	43.2	25.9	38.3	30.0	47.9	38.8	42.1	39.5
40–49 years	30.2	38.2	37.9	39.9	30.6	34.7	33.8	35.0
50–59 years	10.5	25.8	12.7	23.5	7.0	15.0	8.9	17.1
Educational attainment[a]								
Less than high school	2.0	4.8	1.1	2.3	3.6	7.1	1.2	3.5
High school graduate or GED	14.4	25.3	12.6	26.0	12.7	18.2	8.7	21.6
Some college with no degree	48.3	47.3	48.7	46.4	55.3	52.3	43.2	49.6
Bachelor's degree or higher	35.3	22.6	37.6	25.3	28.4	22.4	46.8	25.2
Enrolled in higher education[a]	24.1	10.3	15.2	6.7	20.1	14.8	17.8	11.5
Average number of children	1.6	1.5	1.6	1.5	1.7	1.6	1.6	1.6

SOURCE: ACS-PUMS, five-year file, 2016–2020.

[a] Denotes significant differences by race, ethnicity, and gender within veterans at the < 0.01 level.

TABLE A.14

Racial and Ethnic Differences by Gender in Financial Security Across Veteran Single Parents

Demographic Characteristic	Black, Non-Hispanic		White, Non-Hispanic		Hispanic		Other	
	Women	Men	Women	Men	Women	Men	Women	Men
Median personal income[a]	$35,000	$35,900	$38,000	$50,000	$37,000	$49,600	$36,800	$40,000
Median household income[a]	$47,000	$52,000	$55,000	$67,000	$50,100	$66,000	$58,200	$60,000
Percentage receiving the following forms of assistance								
Self-employment income[a]	3.6	3.6	4.5	6.0	1.5	4.8	4.6	7.3
Supplementary Security Income	2.2	3.3	1.8	2.8	1.7	2.4	1.7	2.7
Public assistance income	3.4	2.9	3.6	2.0	4.1	2.1	3.8	4.1
Retirement income	13.5	12.9	13.3	13.4	12.0	12.1	11.7	10.8
SNAP benefits in last year[a]	27.3	20.4	20.9	12.9	20.9	18.2	18.7	15.6
No health insurance[a]	3.7	5.6	5.5	6.3	3.6	5.9	5.7	12.7
Food security (%)								
Living in a low food security household	21.9	17.9	21.9	11.4	19.8	12.3	42.9	16.5
Living in a very low food security household	8.4	3.1	9.7	2.4	5.5	4.4	17.4	2.2
Receipt of free or reduced-price lunch in last 30 days	22.2	28.4	26.4	15.1	17.9	17.2	34.4	9.8
Use of food pantry in last 30 days[a]	5.1	8.7	13.2	4.7	42.3	9.9	26.8	1.9

SOURCE: ACS-PUMS, five-year file, 2016–2020; CPS-FSS, pooled 2016–2021.

[a] Denotes significant differences by race, ethnicity, and gender within veterans at the < 0.01 level.

TABLE A.15

Racial and Ethnic Differences by Gender in Housing Across Veteran Single Parents

Demographic Characteristic	Black, Non-Hispanic (%)		White, Non-Hispanic (%)		Hispanic (%)		Other (%)	
	Women	Men	Women	Men	Women	Men	Women	Men
Homeownership[a]								
Home owned with mortgage	34.4	33.2	46.7	49.2	37.3	43.9	40.2	37.7
Home owned free and clear	7.3	11.9	12.1	15.0	13.3	13.5	10.3	16.7
Home rented	58.3	54.9	41.3	35.8	49.4	42.6	49.5	45.6
Subfamily household[a]								
Primary household	81.8	77.5	79.7	82.4	83.4	75.0	80.9	74.4
Living in parent household	15.5	18.2	17.3	15.6	13.5	20.8	14.5	22.2
Living in another household	2.7	4.3	3.0	2.0	3.0	4.2	4.6	3.4
Percentage of income spent on housing costs[a]								
< 10%	6.6	7.6	9.5	13.5	8.1	9.6	8.3	14.3
10–19.9%	17.2	24.7	24.2	32.3	19.7	32.4	20.1	23.4
20–29.9%	24.2	21.8	24.2	25.7	17.8	21.8	19.0	21.0
30–39.9%	16.6	16.6	14.8	10.8	17.2	13.2	16.9	14.6
40–49.9%	9.9	7.6	7.6	5.5	8.5	7.7	9.8	7.7
> 50%	22.7	18.1	16.3	10.0	25.1	13.6	22.2	15.6

SOURCE: ACS-PUMS, five-year file, 2016–2020.

[a] Denotes significant differences by race, ethnicity, and gender within veterans at the < 0.01 level.

TABLE A.16

Racial and Ethnic Differences by Gender in Employment Across Veteran Single Parents

Demographic Characteristic	Black, Non-Hispanic		White, Non-Hispanic		Hispanic		Other	
	Women	Men	Women	Men	Women	Men	Women	Men
Employment status (%)[a]								
Currently employed	74.8	73.9	74.8	80.1	74.1	79.2	72.9	78.5
Currently unemployed	5.8	5.4	3.7	5.0	3.9	5.1	6.3	5.4
Not in the labor force	19.4	20.7	21.5	14.9	21.9	15.6	20.8	16.1
Currently employed and enrolled in school[a]	17.3	6.8	9.1	4.5	13.1	10.7	10.4	7.9
Average number of workers in family	1.2	1.1	1.2	1.2	1.2	1.3	1.3	1.3

SOURCE: ACS-PUMS, five-year file, 2016–2020.

[a] Denotes significant differences by race, ethnicity, and gender within veterans at the < 0.01 level.

TABLE A.17

Racial and Ethnic Differences by Gender in Mental and Physical Health Self Ratings Across Veteran Single Parents

Demographic Characteristic	Black, Non-Hispanic		White, Non-Hispanic		Hispanic		Other	
	Women	Men	Women	Men	Women	Men	Women	Men
Mean number of days in the last 30 days with each given health state								
Mental health not good[a]	6.1	4.9	7.2	5.7	8.6	5.1	6.9	7.5
Physical health not good[a]	3.6	4.7	5.4	4.0	4.7	4.4	4.1	5.3
Poor physical or mental health	4.7	6.5	6.2	5.0	7.1	6.5	4.8	5.8
General health status (%)								
Excellent or very good	50.8	54.2	53.2	57.5	48.2	53.7	42.2	49.3
Good	35.7	29.3	32.0	28.7	24.7	29.9	41.6	30.9
Fair or poor	13.6	16.5	14.8	13.8	27.1	16.5	16.2	19.7

SOURCE: BRFSS, pooled 2016–2020.

[a] Denotes significant differences by race, ethnicity, and gender within veterans at the < 0.01 level.

TABLE A.18

Racial and Ethnic Differences by Gender in Access to Health Care Across Veteran Single Parents

Demographic Characteristic	Black, Non-Hispanic (%)		White, Non-Hispanic (%)		Hispanic (%)		Other (%)	
	Women	Men	Women	Men	Women	Men	Women	Men
No health care coverage	9.4	16.1	8.2	12.4	16.7	16.1	6.0	14.7
No personal doctor[a]	21.7	31.4	21.1	37.8	30.7	42.6	21.8	38.8
No routine checkup in last year[a]	17.9	21.2	26.4	34.1	23.5	27.9	21.3	31.1
Could not see doctor in last year because of cost[a]	12.9	16.8	19.1	14.8	24.1	15.1	34.2	11.6

SOURCE: BRFSS, pooled 2016–2020.

[a] Denotes significant differences by race, ethnicity, and gender within veterans at the < 0.01 level.

Abbreviations

ACS	American Community Survey
ACS-PUMS	American Community Survey Public Use Microdata Sample
BRFSS	Behavioral Risk Factor Surveillance System
CDC	Centers for Disease Control and Prevention
COVID-19	coronavirus disease 2019
CPS	Current Population Survey
FSS	Food Security Supplement
GED	General Education Development
SNAP	Supplemental Nutrition Assistance Program
SSI	Social Security Income
VA	U.S. Department of Veterans Affairs
VRC	Veterans Resource Center
WWP	Wounded Warrior Project

References

Adams, Richard E., Yirui Hu, Charles R. Figley, Thomas G. Urosevich, Stuart N. Hoffman, H. Lester Kirchner, Ryan J. Dugan, Joseph J. Boscarino, Carrie A. Withey, and Joseph A. Boscarino, "Risk and Protective Factors Associated with Mental Health Among Female Military Veterans: Results from the Veterans' Health Study," *BioMed Central Women's Health*, Vol. 21, No. 1, February 8, 2021.

Andersen, S. A., ed., "Core Indicators of Nutritional State for Difficult to Sample Populations," *Journal of Nutrition*, Vol. 120, 1990.

Angrist, Joshua D., "The Effect of Veterans Benefits on Education and Earnings," *Industrial and Labor Relations Review*, Vol. 46, No. 4, July 1993.

Bishu, Sebawit G., and Mohamad G. Alkadry, "A Systematic Review of the Gender Pay Gap and Factors That Predict It," *Administration & Society*, Vol. 49, No. 1, 2017.

Bowen, Gary L., Dennis K. Orthner, and Laura I. Zimmerman, "Family Adaptation of Single Parents in the United States Army: An Empirical Analysis of Work Stressors and Adaptive Resources," *Family Relations*, Vol. 42, No. 3, July 1993.

Cairney, John, Michael Boyle, David R. Offord, and Yvonne Racine, "Stress, Social Support and Depression in Single and Married Mothers," *Social Psychiatry and Psychiatric Epidemiology*, Vol. 38, No. 8, August 2003.

Cairney, John, C. Thorpe, J. Rietschlin, and W. R. Avison, "12-Month Prevalence of Depression Among Single and Married Mothers in the 1994 National Population Health Survey," *Canadian Journal of Public Health*, Vol. 90, No. 5, 1999.

Carlson, Marie, Maurice Endlsey, Darnell Motley, Lamise N. Shawahin, and Monnica T. Williams, "Addressing the Impact of Racism on Veterans of Color: A Race-Based Stress and Trauma Intervention," *Psychology of Violence*, Vol. 8, No. 6, 2018.

Coles, Roberta L. "Single-Father Families: A Review of the Literature," *Journal of Family Theory & Review*, Vol. 7, No. 2, June 2015.

Consumer Financial Protection Bureau Office of Servicemember Affairs, *Financial Well-Being of Veterans*, April 2019.

Craig, Lyn, "The Money or the Care: A Comparison of Couple and Sole Parent Households' Time Allocation to Work and Children," *Australian Journal of Social Issues*, Vol. 40, No. 4, 2006.

Davies, Lorraine, William R. Avison, and Donna D. McAlpine, "Significant Life Experiences and Depression Among Single and Married Mothers, *Journal of Marriage and Family*, Vol. 59, No. 2, May 1997.

Dubowitz, Tamara, *Food Insecurity Among Veterans: Veterans' Issues in Focus*, RAND Corporation, PE-A1363-2, 2021. As of October 30, 2023: https://www.rand.org/pubs/perspectives/PEA1363-2.html

Gault, Barbara, Jessica Milli, and Lindsey Reichlin Cruse, *Investing in Single Mothers' Higher Education: Costs and Benefits to Individuals, Families, and Society*, Institute for Women's Policy Research, June 6, 2018.

Ghaleiha, Amin, Carrie Barber, Armon J. Tamatea, and Amy Bird, "Fathers' Help Seeking Behavior and Attitudes During Their Transition to Parenthood, *Infant Mental Health Journal*, Vol. 43, No. 5, 2022.

Gorman, Bridget K., and Jennifer Braverman, "Family Structure Differences in Health Care Utilization Among US Children," *Social Science & Medicine*, Vol. 67, No. 11, 2008.

Hall, Lauren, "SNAP Helps 1.2 Million Low-Income Veterans, Including Thousands in Every State," Center on Budget and Policy Priorities, November 9, 2021.

Hanson, Devlin, and Tyler Woods, *The State of Post-9/11 Veteran Families*, Urban Institute Center on Labor, Human Services, and Population, November 2016.

Hepburn, Peter, "Parental Work Schedules and Child-Care Arrangements in Low-Income Families, *Journal of Marriage and Family*, Vol. 80, No. 5, June 22, 2018.

Holder, Kelly Ann, "Post-9/11 Women Veterans," presentation, Annual Meeting of the Population Association of America, 2010.

Horne, Rebecca M., Matthew D. Johnson, Nancy L. Galambos, and Harvey J. Krahn, "Time, Money, or Gender? Predictors of the Division of Household Labour Across Life Stages," *Sex Roles*, Vol. 78, 2018.

Jayakody, Rukmalie, and Dawn Stauffer, "Mental Health Problems Among Single Mothers: Implications for Work and Welfare Reform," *Journal of Social Issues*, Vol. 56, No. 4, December 17, 2002.

Johnson, Anna D., and Anna J. Markowitz, "Food Insecurity and Family Well-Being Outcomes Among Households with Young Children," *Journal of Pediatrics*, Vol. 196, May 2018.

Kalil, Ariel, and Kathleen M. Ziol-Guest, "Single Mothers' Employment Dynamics and Adolescent Well-Being," *Child Development*, Vol. 76, No. 1, 2005.

Kimberlin, Sara, *California's Housing Affordability Crisis Hits Renters and Households with the Lowest Incomes the Hardest*, California Budget and Policy Center, April 2019.

Livingston, Gretchen, *The Rise of Single Fathers: A Ninefold Increase Since 1960*, Pew Research Center, July 2, 2013.

Lleras, Christy, "Employment, Work Conditions, and the Home Environment in Single-Mother Families, *Journal of Family Issues*, Vol. 29, No. 10, February 28, 2008.

Mattingly, Marybeth J., Kristin Smith, and Jessica A. Bean, "Unemployment in the Great Recession: Single Parents and Men Hit Hard," Carsey School of Public Policy, University of New Hampshire, August 31, 2011.

McLaughlin, Ruth, Lisa Nielsen, and Michael Waller, "An Evaluation of the Effect of Military Service on Mortality: Quantifying the Healthy Soldier Effect," *Annals of Epidemiology*, Vol. 18, No. 12, 2008.

Military OneSource, "2021 Demographics Dashboards: Interactive Profile of the Military Community," webpage, undated. As of October 30, 2023: https://demographics.militaryonesource.mil/

Monheit, Alan C., Irina Grafova, and Rizie Kumar, "How Does Family Health Care Use Respond to Economic Shocks? Realized and Anticipated Effects," *Review of Economics of the Household*, Vol. 18, 2020.

Nam, Suk Kyung, Hui Jung Chu, Mi Kyoung Lee, Ji Hee Lee, Nuri Kim, and Sang Min Lee, "A Meta-Analysis of Gender Differences in Attitudes Toward Seeking Professional Psychological Help," *Journal of American College Health*, Vol. 59, No. 2, 2010.

Ozhamaratli, Fatih, Oleg Kitov, and Paolo Barucca, "A Generative Model for Age and Income Distribution, *EPJ Data Science*, Vol. 11, No. 1, January 29, 2022.

Pearlin, L. I., and J. S. Johnson, "Marital Status, Life-Strains and Depression," *American Sociological Review*, Vol. 42, No. 5, October 1977.

Pooler, Jennifer A., Mithuna Srinivasan, Paula Mian, and Zachary Miller, "Prevalence and Risk Factors for Food Insecurity Among Low-Income US Military Veterans," *Public Health Reports*, Vol. 136, No. 5, 2021.

Ramchand, Rajeev, Terri Tanielian, Michael P. Fisher, Christine Anne Vaughan, Thomas E. Trail, Caroline Epley, Phoenix Voorhies, Michael William Robbins, Eric Robinson, and Bonnie Ghosh-Dastidar, *Hidden Heroes: America's Military Caregivers*, RAND Corporation, RR-499-TEDF, 2014. As of May 30, 2023:
https://www.rand.org/pubs/research_reports/RR499.html

Robinson, Lori, and Michael E. O'Hanlon, "Women Warriors: The Ongoing Story of Integrating and Diversifying the American Armed Forces," Brookings Institute, 2020.

"Servicemen's Readjustment Act (1944)," webpage, National Archives, undated. As of December 15, 2023:
https://www.archives.gov/milestone-documents/servicemens-readjustment-act

Sheppard, Sean C., Jennifer W. Malatras, and Allen C. Israel, "The Impact of Deployment on U.S. Military Families, *American Psychologist*, Vol. 65, No. 6, 2010.

Yi, Stacey, and Sierra Smucker, *Meeting the Changing Needs of Veterans: Insights from Student Veterans Who Are Single Parents*, RAND Corporation, RB-A1363-2, 2024.

Tanielian, Terri, Lisa H. Jaycox, Terry L. Schell, Grant N. Marshall, M. Audrey Burnam, Christine Eibner, Benjamin R. Karney, Lisa S. Meredith, Jeanne S. Ringel, Mary E. Vaiana, and the Invisible Wounds Study Team, *Invisible Wounds of War: Summary and Recommendations for Addressing Psychological and Cognitive Injuries*, RAND Corporation, MG-720/1-CCF, 2008. As of October 30, 2023:
https://www.rand.org/pubs/monographs/MG720z1.html

Trautmann, Jennifer, Jeanne Alhusen, and Deborah Gross, "Impact of Deployment on Military Families with Young Children: A Systematic Review," *Nursing Outlook*, Vol. 63, No. 6, 2015.

U.S. Department of Veterans Affairs, "GI Bill Comparison Tool," webpage, undated-b. As of July 23, 2023:
https://www.va.gov/education/gi-bill-comparison-tool/

U.S. Department of Veterans Affairs, "Post 9-11 GI Bill (Chapter 33) Rates," webpage, undated-c. As of July 28, 2023:
https://www.va.gov/education/benefit-rates/post-9-11-gi-bill-rates/

U.S. Department of Veterans Affairs, *Women Veterans Report: The Past, Present, and Future of Women Veterans*, February 2017.

VA—*See* U.S. Department of Veterans Affairs.

Wang, Jian Li, "The Difference Between Single and Married Mothers in the 12-Month Prevalence of Major Depression Syndrome, Associated Factors and Mental Health Service Utilization," *Social Psychiatry and Psychiatric Epidemiology*, Vol. 39, No. 1, January 2004.

Wounded Warrior Project, *Women Warriors Initiative Report*, 2021.

Wu, Chi Fang, and Mary Keegan Eamon, "Patterns and Correlates of Involuntary Unemployment and Underemployment in Single-Mother Families, *Children and Youth Services Review*, Vol. 33, No. 6, June 2011.

WWP—*See* Wounded Warrior Project.

Milton Keynes UK
Ingram Content Group UK Ltd.
UKHW020312200324
439698UK00022B/578